God's Law
in the
New Covenant

By

Stephen M. Siefken

Dedication

This book is dedicated to the one true lawgiver, judge, and King of the Universe (Is. 33:22) for the restoration of His commandments in the nations of today.

Verses of Inspiration

"And many nations shall come, and say, Come, and let us go up to the mountain of YHVH, and to the house of the God of Jacob; and he will teach us of his ways, and we will walk in his paths: for the law shall go forth of Zion, and the word of YHVH from Jerusalem."

Micah 4:2

"The fear of YHVH is the beginning of wisdom: a good understanding have all they that do his commandments: his praise endures forever."

Psalms 111:10

For the commandment is a lamp; and the law is light; and reproofs of instruction are the way of life:

Prov. 6:23

"Blessed are the undefiled in the way, who walk in the law of YHVH. Blessed are they that keep his testimonies, and that seek him with the whole heart."

Psalms 119:1-2

God's Law in the New Covenant
The Torah in the Nations
Book One

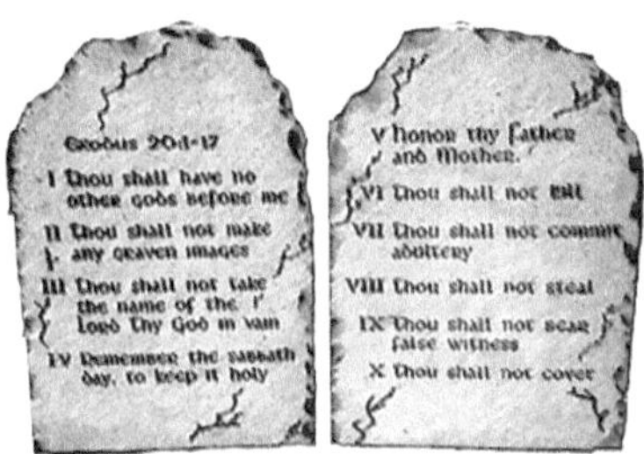

By Stephen M. Siefken

Answereth a Matter
www.answerethamatter.org
proverbs1813@att.net
P.O. Box 244, Aguanga, CA 92536, USA

Table of Contents

About the Author

Steve Siefken is a husband and a father who resides in Southern California. He has been a teacher in public school for the past twenty-eight years and an active participant at every church he has attended. He started his walk following the Messiah in 1992 at the age of nineteen. He quickly became involved assisting and teaching in the College and Career Bible Study at his local church. At the same time, he also changed his college focus to Education and Biblical Studies earning a Bachelor of Arts degree in Kinesiology and Health Promotion and a minor in Biblical Studies at Pacific Christian College. He then earned his teaching credential at California State University of Fullerton and followed this with a Master of Education degree from Hope International University, formerly Pacific Christian College.

In 2005, he started his first website to host his personal Bible studies and commentary at the request of his wife, Rachelle. She saw how much time and effort Steve put into his study of the scripture and thought others might want to glean from his work. This website is still growing today and is called Answereth a Matter (www.answerethamatter.org). Steve wrote many articles and answered several email questions about such articles. Shortly thereafter, his focus became more and more on teaching the Bible to other believers. He started assisting the junior high and high school ministries by teaching junior high Awana and a junior high VBS with his wife. He also joined a street witnessing ministry going door to door sharing the gospel to his local community.

In 2008, he was challenged with the Torah, or the Law of God. This completely changed his outlook on the entire scripture and caused him to take a very deep look into the first five books of the Bible. After categorizing and organizing the entire Torah into titles of law, it became clear that God's law was still for people today. He started attending a Sabbath keeping church and started teaching seminars at their Feast of Tabernacles celebrations. At this point, his wife, Rachelle, again encouraged him to start a YouTube Channel and record his teachings. It took nearly eight years, but the result of all his Torah studies produced a ten-part series of lessons that became popular on his YouTube Channel, eventually giving rise to an invitation to Shabbat Night Live with Michael Rood. Since this invitation, he has been invited back multiple times and his YouTube channel and website have increased in popularity.

Steve is most noted for his unique perspective on the Mosaic Law. This perspective provides a very practical reason for each of God's commandments and an organizational structure modeled after modern law and the Messiah's own words saying, "On these two commandments hang all the law and the prophets" (Matt. 22:40). This unique perspective demonstrates the importance of keeping God's commandments in every nation today. Steve's purpose today is to share this perspective to the churches of America and demonstrate the need for nations to keep the commandments of God.

Preface

I started walking with the Messiah in 1992. I took the Bible very seriously and studied as much as possible. I led small Bible studies from time to time, but these were usually very casual and mostly discussion based. The first time I really taught the scriptures in an organized manner was in 2009. My wife and I volunteered to teach the junior high Awana class. Since we were both teachers, we did what teachers typically do. We used the lesson as a guide and developed our own lesson instead. We always put together a PowerPoint presentation from the Awana book, but we added as much scriptural detail as we could so the students would learn as much as they were capable of. One of these Awana lessons was about the Law of God. The point of the lesson was simple, God gave us a perfect standard that we could not meet. Luckily for us, Jesus met the standard so we didn't have to. This is a typical theological point for most churches today. Jesus did away with the law because we couldn't keep it, and I whole heartedly believed this.

In my PowerPoint lesson, I scrolled through all 613 commandments so everyone could see them listed out. At the end of the slide I said, "Jesus fulfilled all these so we no longer have to keep them." This, after all, was what I believed. What happened next, I was not prepared for. One child was paying attention and asked the question, do we still have to keep the Ten Commandments since they were at the beginning of the list? My quick response was an emphatic, "No. Jesus fulfilled all the law. We no longer have to keep them." After all, this is what I believed. That same student then asked, what about murder? As I paused to ponder the question, I quickly realized that I had painted myself into a difficult corner to get out of. I quickly changed the subject and moved on in the lesson, but I could not rationalize what I believed in my own mind.

This led me on a pursuit to understand the Law of God so I could give a better answer to this question. Little did I know that it would change how I saw the entire Bible. The Law of God is one of the most neglected portions of the Holy Scripture. It is often only taught as a law for ancient Israel, if taught at all. I was not aware of the magnitude of impact this would have on my interpretation of the Holy Scriptures. The foundation of all the scripture lies within the first five books called the Torah. Unfortunately, the Torah is highly overshadowed by modern New Testament theology. As I delved deep into the study of God's law it quickly became apparent that my New Testament theology was flawed.

Since that time, I have been on a pursuit to understand God's law through His eyes. I started by writing out a copy of the Torah with my own hand. This is what God asked the kings of Israel to do (Deut. 17:18), so I thought it would be a good place to start. After that, I went through God's law again and categorized each commandment into titles of law. Then, I placed each title of law under one or more of the Ten Commandments, and I divided the Ten Commandments under the two greatest commandments, to love God and to love your neighbor. After all, this is what the Messiah said, "On these two commandments hang all the law and the prophets" (Matt. 22:40). It took nearly ten years, but I went through the entirety of the Mosaic law and organized it the way the Messiah taught. This led to the development of a ten-part series of lessons going through every commandment of the scripture that I was privileged to teach in 2017. This book series is the culmination of that work and is designed to demonstrate the importance of keeping every commandment of God within our lives and nations today.

> **Matthew 22:37-40**
>
> Jesus said unto him, Thou shalt love the Lord thy God with all thy heart, and with all thy soul, and with all thy mind. This is the first and great commandment. And the second is like unto it, Thou shalt love thy neighbor as thyself. On these two commandments hang all the law and the prophets.

- **756 Commandments, Statutes, and Judgments**
- **87 Titles of Law**
- **10 Commandments**
- **2 Greatest Commandments**

	Love the LORD your God					Love your neighbor as yourself				
	1	**2**	**3**	**4**	**5**	**6**	**7**	**8**	**9**	**10**
	You shall have no other gods before me.	You shall make no graven images.	You shall not take the name of the LORD in vain.	Remember the Sabbath day, to keep it holy.	Honor your father and mother.	You shall not murder.	You shall not commit adultery.	You shall not steal.	You shall not bear false witness.	You shall not covet your neighbor's possessions.
Titles of Law	- Court Policies (22) - Faith (4) - Fear of God (9) - Firstborn (8) - First Fruits (4) - Foreign Policy (9) - Kings (6) - Nazarite Vow (6) - Law of Land (6) - Obedience (4) - Offerings Burnt (13) - Offerings Drink (4) - Offerings Heave (12) -Offerings Meat (9) -Offerings Peace (17) -Offerings Wave (11) - Priesthood Aaronic (22) - Priesthood High Priest (16) - Priesthood Levitical (9) - Tithing First (10) - War (31)	- Appearance (8) - Idolatry (10) - Public (5)	- Backsliding (3) - Blasphemy (3) - Blessings (31) - Circumcision (3) - Curses (34) - Government (10) - Head Tax (4) - Judges (16) - Judgment (5) - Offerings Sin (17) - Offerings Trespass (8) - Prophets (6) - Punishment (21) - Repentance (3) - Reproof (2) - Vengeance (2) - Witchcraft (3)	- Feast Passover (36) - Feast Unleavened Bread (11) - Feast First Fruits (7) - Feast Weeks (9) - Feast Trumpets (6) - Feast Atonement (31) -Feast Tabernacle (10) - Feast 8th Day (3) - New Moon (6) - Sabbath (9) - Tithing Second (7)	- Education (4) - Family (6)	- Agriculture (6) - Animals (10) -Bearing Children (8) -Clean & Unclean (10) - Diet/Health (7) - Healing (10) - Manslaughter (6) - Menstruation (8) - Murder (8) - Sanitation (14)	- Adultery (12) - Divorce (7) - Marriage (18)	- Bribery (1) - Business (10) - Charity (10) - Contracts (12) - Disability (2) - Fraud (2) - Inheritance (5) - Land (8) - Land Sabbath (7) - Money (2) - Negligence (5) - Restitution (22) - Servant/Hired (3) - Servants/Bond (9) - Slavery (7) - Theft (3) - Tithing Third (4) - Usury (2) - Year Jubilee (5)	-Perjury (2)	- Intent (8)

An example of the Mosaic Law codified as the Messiah described. Created by author.

Also available at www.answerethamatter.org/PDF/Mosaic_Law_Overview.pdf

Chapter One

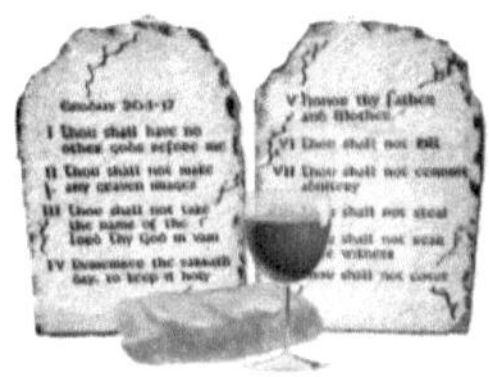

Introduction

One of the most prominent traits of the modern church today is the belief that the Law of God is no longer relevant. This modern belief says that faith in the Messiah gives grace. As a result, one is no longer under the law, but under grace (Rom. 6:14). Somehow, the gospel message has dismissed the law and only grace remains. Although this is probably one of the most prevalent church beliefs today, is this what the church has always believed? Better yet, is this what the Scriptures teach? This three-book series will take a deep dive into the Law of God to better understand its purpose for today and will tackle some very difficult topics such as the Sacrificial System and the Levitical Priesthood. This first book, however, will focus primarily on the interpretation of God's law and the misconception today that it is no longer relevant. It will finish with a practical explanation as to where God's law is today and under what law system it can be found. The belief that God's law has been abolished and replaced with grace can be very dangerous. In fact, this belief is only growing stronger today. However, there are pockets of believers across the world that believe God's law is relevant today and this movement is growing more and more.

This belief that God's law no longer applies today is called Antinomianism and was rejected by the early church fathers. An Antinomian is "one who holds that under the gospel dispensation of grace the moral law is of no use or obligation because faith alone is necessary to salvation."[1] Although this is a prominent teaching today, is this what the Scriptures actually teach? The truth is, God did give His Law and that Law was said to be forever hundreds of times in the Scripture (Ex. 27:21, Lev. 16:29, Num. 15:15, Deut. 12:28, Matt. 5:17-19, etc.). Was God wrong? Why did He say "forever" if He did not mean "forever?" God must have had a reason for giving His Law, but what was it? To answer these questions, it is important to turn to the Scripture. After all, the, "Scripture is [not] of any private interpretation" (2 Pet. 1:20). It is important to understand the place of God's law from His perspective and not man's. Afterall, God is the author of the Scripture; it is His interpretation that ultimately matters. Since God warned us hundreds, even thousands of times in the Scripture, this is a vitally important topic to consider. Even the Messiah warned us of ignoring this topic. In Matthew 24, the Messiah is warning His disciples concerning the last days. He warns them of "false prophets" who will "deceive

---

[1] "Antinomian." Merriam-Webster.com Dictionary, Merriam-Webster, https://www.merriam-webster.com/dictionary/antinomian. Accessed 5 Nov 2018.

many." In verse eleven the Messiah states, "And many false prophets shall rise, and shall deceive many." In the last days there will be false prophets that will preach deception. The question to ask is simple, what is this deception? He answers this in the very next verse. In verse twelve He states, "And because iniquity shall abound, the love of many shall wax cold." The word iniquity is the Greek word anomia which literally means, "the condition of one without law".[2] The Messiah warns us to beware of false prophets (false preachers) who deceive many. The result of their deception is lawlessness. Isn't this exactly what today's church is preaching? It seems the number one doctrine taught in churches today is that we are "under grace" and not "under law." Their understanding of not being "under the law" is that we no longer need to practice God's law, but is this the correct understanding? Perhaps we should be aware of the Messiah's warning and, "Test all things; [and] hold fast that which is good" (1 Thess. 5:21). After all, this is what the Apostle Paul told us to do. We are to test everything. The purpose of this first book of the series is to explore the place of God's law in the New Covenant and examine how that law should be used today. First, however, some basic terminology needs to be addressed for clarity.

Terminology:

It is important to address some basic concepts before moving forward. There are many different types of

---

[2] Thayer, Joseph H. "Anomia." *Thayer's Greek - English Lexicon of the New Testament,* 11th ed., Baker Book House, 2014, pp. 48–48.

terminology used in churches today. For example, the most common name used in America for the Messiah of Israel is Jesus. However, many who practice God's law prefer to use the Hebrew name Yeshua. Another example is the name of God. The name of God is the Hebrew word YHVH. This is translated as "the LORD" in most Bible translations. Although it is clear that "the LORD" is not the correct translation, it is not very clear what the correct translation should be. The true name of God is debated in many circles of Christianity today, but one thing that is clear is the fact that no one really knows God's true name. These differences in terminology can cause much confusion. As a result, for the sake of clarity, this book will use the most common terminology in the mainstream church of America, but with a few exceptions. For the name of God, the tetragrammaton (YHVH), will be used and for the name Yeshua/Jesus, the title Messiah will be used unless it is used in a quote. Please do not construe this as an insult in any way. This book is written for the purpose of providing clarity regarding the Law of God. Using terminology that is unknown or confusing will only distract from that purpose. Whenever a mainstream word is used that distracts from an important truth, an explanation will be given and a better word will be used. This is an attempt to provide as much clarity as possible for a wider audience of readers.

The biblical text that will be quoted the most will be the King James Version. This version is in the public domain in the United States and free to use as one sees fit. Most of the quotes in this writing will use the King James version so that this author has the freedom to change a word from time to time for clarity. The most often change will be the removal of Old English words for a more modern word to avoid confusion. When a change is made from Old English to modern English no notation will be made. Sometimes a word will be changed to add clarification based on a point that this author is trying to make. When this is done the word will be placed in brackets []. When a different translation is quoted it will be noted with the abbreviation of that specific translation.

Assumptions:

Another distraction that is common is when an author does not disclose their assumptions. Every writer has their own assumptions. This is the natural effect of having the freedom to think. An assumption is something that is accepted as true without providing evidence or proof. An author might believe something and write as if it is accepted even though the book is not covering that specific topic. This is an absolute necessity to help a book keep its focus on the topic at hand, but it is helpful for the reader to understand these assumptions. It seems best that these assumptions are disclosed so the reader can better understand the perspective of the author. With that said, here are some assumptions this author will have when writing this book.

1. The Law of God is good for us. God said it was "for our good always, that he might preserve us alive, as it is at this day" (Deut. 6:24). The Scripture always portrays God's law in a very positive manner. Just because a commandment is hard to understand does not mean it should be rejected. When understood through God's eyes it will be

clear that it is for our good. The modern belief that God's law is a burden is simply not true and nowhere stated in the Scripture. However, the opposite is stated numerous times.

2. The Law of God is what defines righteous living. "And it shall be our righteousness, if we observe to do all these commandments before YHVH our God, as he has commanded us" (Deut. 6:25). God's law does not give people their righteousness, but it does define what righteousness is. Man's righteousness comes only from the Messiah (2 Cor. 5:21), but the Messiah's righteousness looks just like obedience to God's law. Afterall, the Messiah fulfilled all the law and the prophets (Matt. 5:17).

3. The only way to understand God's law is to do God's law. Psalm 111:10 says, "The fear of YHVH is the beginning of wisdom: a good understanding have all they that do his commandments: his praise endures forever." This is also echoed in the New Testament when James said, "But be ye doers of the word, and not hearers only, deceiving your own selves" (James 1:22). Deception is the opposite of understanding. We can only understand the benefit of God's law by the practice of God's law.

4. When studying the Mosaic Law, we need to remember that it is a law and not a religion. Many times, we don't understand God's law because we are studying it as a religion. The truth is that it is a law and needs to be studied as a lawyer would study law.

5. Israel was a nation and not a church. It is a mistake to compare Israel to the church today. We need to compare Israel with other nations and not churches. God's law is a national law and this law was built for nations to follow. This book will focus on comparing God's law to all nations, and specifically America.

6. The Law of God is compared to a mirror and should be used to look back at ourselves, not towards others. The Apostle James said, "But be ye doers of the word, and not hearers only, deceiving your own selves. For if any be a hearer of the word, and not a doer, he is like unto a man beholding his natural face in a glass: For he beholds himself, and goes his way, and straightway forgets what manner of man he was. But whoso looks into the perfect law of liberty, and continues therein, he being not a forgetful hearer, but a doer of the work, this man shall be blessed in his deed" (James 1:22-25). Believers are to compare their lives to the Law of God. When it reveals a flaw in the believer's life then a change in that life is needed. This is the purpose of God's law. It helps us correct the behavior in our lives.

7. There are cultural differences throughout the history of mankind. Many times, these cultural differences cause scriptural interpretation to be unclear. It is important to understand the writings of the Scripture based upon the culture of the time it was written. As a result, throughout this series this writer will use historical writings such as Josephus, Philo, and early church fathers to better understand the culture of biblical times. It is important to remember that their writings are not Scripture and in no way should be treated on the

same level as the Scripture. These writings only serve to better understand the times of their day. Their doctrine, however, is always subject to error.

These are some of the assumptions made at the writing of this book. Each assumption is based on scriptural principles. It is important to understand the Scripture the way the readers and writers would have understood. This means that the student of Scripture needs to understand the times of the writing as well as the meaning of the words they used. Many times, we use our own personal presuppositions to interpret the Scripture. It is important to remove these presuppositions and accept what the readers and writers of that time period would have understood. This is what this writer calls a scriptural mindset. It is incredibly important to have the mindset that the people of the time of the writing would have had. This is the only way to truly understand what the Scripture is speaking of. This is why the next chapter is titled, "How to Study the Scripture". It is important to have a systematic method of how to study the Scripture and only fair for an author to disclose that method. The next chapter contains the method of study used to make the conclusions in this book.

Chapter Two

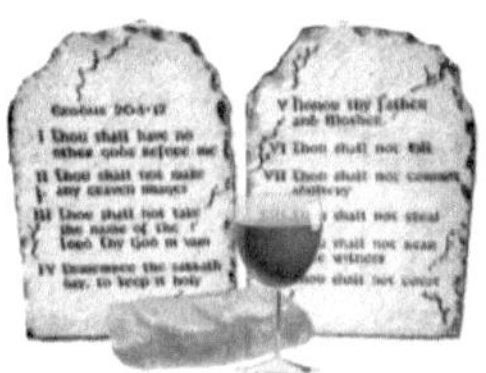

How to Study the Scripture

One of the biggest problems in the church today is the lack of real biblical study. Sermons typically consist of a feel-good message designed to tickle the ears of the congregation. Some pastors might deliver a sermon to convict the people, but rarely do we see any real study of the Scripture. Many in the congregation might study the Scripture themselves, but all too often what is called "Bible Study" is simply a casual read of the Scripture. Those that do take the time to really study the Scripture often have no real method of study. Very few church members systematically study the Bible using the method of study found in the Scripture. This chapter is designed to highlight the scriptural standards for biblical study. Most of the problems we find in the Scripture are answered when we use scriptural principles of biblical study.

The Bible tells us to, "Study to show yourself approved unto God, a workman that needs not to be ashamed, rightly dividing the word of truth" (2 Tim 2:15). The big question is: How do we "rightly divide the word of truth?" This is very important because believers are to worship the Father in "spirit and truth" (John 4:24). And what is truth? "Thy word is truth" (John 17:17). It is important to not only worship the Father, but to also seek out the truth of His word. The question to answer in this chapter is this: How are believers to study the Scripture, and specifically, study the Law of God?

The Apostle Peter helps answer this question. In 2 Peter 1:20, the apostle states, "Knowing this first, that no prophecy of the Scripture is of any private interpretation." The Scripture is not to be interpreted man's way, but God's way. Believers are not to interpret the Scripture at all, but rather, let the Scripture interpret the Scripture. The next logical question is, how do believers let the Scripture interpret the Scripture? Did God tell believers how to understand His word? Believe it or not, He did. The Scripture actually teaches how it is organized and how to study. According to Isaiah 28:9-14 the Scripture is written in legal code. This should not be a surprise for all law is written in legal code. Just as the Constitution is the law of this land so the Bible is the Law of God. And what is legal code? As Isaiah states in Isaiah 28:10, "For precept must be upon precept, precept upon precept; line upon line, line upon line; here a little, and there a little." This is a perfect example of legal code. Whenever law is codified, it is done in this manner. It is codified in a systematic "line upon line" and "precept upon precept." As the law code grows, each topic is spread throughout the code "here a little, and there a little." Afterall, this is what codification means: "Codification is the process of compiling rules and laws into an orderly, formal code. The code is a systematic compilation of existing laws to be included in a legislative statute."[3] Law is organized orderly and systematically. The Bible is organized the same way. The Bible is a law book and needs to be studied as law. It needs to be studied as a lawyer would study to prepare his case for trial.

The Bible as a Law Book:

Looking at the Scripture as a law book might seem strange, but consider some of the Hebrew words that describe God's law.

- צָוָה - Tsâvâh – H6680 – This is the word for command. It means "to constitute, enjoin, appoint or give charge."[4] This is the word God used when He ratified the covenant with Moses and the Israelites.
- מִצְוָה - Mitzvah – H4687 – This word is most often translated commandments. This word is defined as, "a command - law, ordinance, or precept."[5] This is a chief command or law.
- חֹק - Chôq – H2706 – This word is most often translated as statutes. This word means, "an enactment - commandment, custom, decree, or

---

[3] Wex Definitions Team, Wex Legal Information Institute, Cornell Law School, "Codification." August of 2022, obtained July, 28, 2024, https://www.law.cornell.edu/wex/codification

[4] Strong, James, "Command – צָוָה - tsâvâh." *A Concise Dictionary of the Words in the Hebrew Bible*, pg. 98, H6680.

[5] Strong, James, "Commandments – מִצְוָה - mitzvah." *A Concise Dictionary of the Words in the Hebrew Bible*, pg. 71, H4687.

ordinance."[6] This refers to a lesser commandment that helps define a greater commandment.

- מִשְׁפָּט - Mishpâṭ – H4941 – This is the word for judgments. This word means, "a verdict, pronounced judicially, especially a sentence or formal decree."[7] This refers to a judge construing a law by giving a sentence at trial. When a judge construes a law this now becomes the standard for construing that law. This is done to help add clarification to laws that might be vague or ambiguous.
- לֶקַח – Leqach - H3948 and διδαχή – didache - G1322 - The Hebrew word leqach and the Greek word didache are usually translated as doctrines. These two words mean, "instruction, doctrine, learning." [8] [9] Doctrines are not considered law, but rather are rules or principles of law to help determine judgments.
- תּוֹרָה - Tôrâh – H8451 – This is the word translated as law in the Scripture. This word means, "law, directions, or instruction, a precept or statute".[10] It refers specifically to the "Decalogue or Pentateuch."[11] This is the word that represents all of God's law.

---

[6] Strong, James, "Statute – חֹק - chôq." *A Concise Dictionary of the Words in the Hebrew Bible*, pg. 42, H2706.

[7] Strong, James, "Judgments – מִשְׁפָּט - mishpâṭ." *A Concise Dictionary of the Words in the Hebrew Bible*, pg. 74, H4941.

[8] Strong, James, "Doctrines – לֶקַח - leqach." *A Concise Dictionary of the Words in the Hebrew Bible*, pg. 60, H3948.

[9] Strong, James, "Doctrines – διδαχή - didache." *A Concise Dictionary of the Words in the Greek Bible*, pg. 23, G1322

[10] F. Brown, S. Driver, and C. Briggs, "Law – תּוֹרָה - tôrâh." *The Brown-Driver-Briggs Hebrew and English Lexicon*, pg. 435, H8451.

[11] Strong, James, "Law – תּוֹרָה - tôrâh." *A Concise Dictionary of the Words in the Hebrew Bible*, pg. 123, H8451.

To put this in modern terms a comparison can be made between Ancient Israel and the United States of America. Tsavah is the Ten Commandments where the law was enjoined or commanded for Israel. In the United States, tsavah is the Constitution. This is where the United States law was enjoined or commanded. Mitzvah and choq represent the commandments and statutes. This represents the law placed on the side of the Ark of the Covenant in ancient Israel (Deut. 31:26). In America, this would represent the United States Code and the many statutes under our constitution. Mishpaṭ represents all of the judgments from Hebrew courts. In America, it represents the judgments from our Federal and State courts. Leqach and didache represent biblical doctrines of law. Doctrines of law are instructions on how to construe law. In America, this represents the Cannons of Construction on how to construe legal documents. All of these words are represented in the word Torah, which is law. In fact, it is commonly taught that Torah means instructions, however, instructions is a poor understanding of Torah. Although, instructions are part of God's law, for all law is instructive, this is only part of the definition. The word law is still the best translation for Torah. The problem is a lack of understanding of what law really means. According to Bouvier's Law Dictionary, law is "a solemn expression of the legislative will."[12] Similarly, according to Black's Law Dictionary, "Law is a solemn expression of legislative will."[13] Since God is the legislature of the Torah, then Torah is the solemn expression of God's

____

[12] Bouvier, John, "Law." *A Law Dictionary Adapted to the Constitution and Laws of the United States of America*, Vol. II, pg. 7.

[13] Black, Henry Campbell, "Law." *Black's Law Dictionary*, Fifth Edition, pg. 795.

will. This is the best definition of Torah that this writer can think of. Instructions fall short of a complete definition of Torah. For example, instructions do not have penalties, but God's law clearly has penalties and law today contains penalties as well. The word law is still the best definition of Torah in the English language.

To further understand this concept, compare the Bible to other forms of law. A comparison between biblical law and the United States law will be an excellent example. The United States started with the Law of the Land (U.S. Constitution), added to it were several statutes (U.S. Code), and finally all the judgments through the years from our courts. From this come several Doctrines of Law such as stare decicis, due process, or burden of proof. This is the law of the United States. The Bible is written the same way. The Law of God started with the Law of the Land which is the Ten Commandments inside the Ark of the Covenant (Ex. 40:20), added to it were over seven hundred statutes placed outside of the Ark of the Covenant (Deut. 31:26), and finally there are several judgments decided by the Hebrew courts such as the daughters of Zelophehad (Num. 27:1-11). From this come several Doctrines of Law such as baptism, justification, and sanctification, none of which could exist apart from God's law. The problem for most believers is they study biblical doctrines without understanding biblical law. This writer contends that you cannot understand these doctrines without first understanding the law behind them. See Table 1 to help understand this comparison.

A Comparison of Two Nations	
United States	Ancient Israel
• Constitution	• 10 Commandments (tsavah)
• US Code	• Hundreds of statutes on the side of the ark (mitzvah/choq)
• Many US court decisions	• Hebrew court decisions (mishpaṭ)

• Many doctrines of law
  o Stare decisis, due process, burden of proof
	• Many doctrines of law (leqach/didache)
	  o Baptism, resurrection, sanctification

• Legal definitions are defined inside the statute	• Biblical definitions are defined inside the Bible

Table 1

With this legal mindset it is easier to understand how to study God's word. The first step in understanding the Scripture is to understand each passage's immediate context. As Isaiah said in Isaiah 28:10, "For precept must be upon precept, precept upon precept; line upon line, line upon line." This is an appeal to correct context. The Scripture must be studied, "line upon line" and "precept upon precept". However, this is just the start. Once the context of a passage is understood, this only gives part of the overall picture the Scripture portrays. The next part of Isaiah 28:10 is, "here a little, and there a little." This suggests that there might be more on this topic, "here" in this section of Scripture, or, "there" in that section of Scripture. Once the context of a passage is understood it is imperative to search the rest of the Scripture to see if God said more on the specific topic being studied.

Here are a few examples. Romans 6:4 is a great passage to study when trying to understand the doctrine of baptism; however, there are dozens of other passages that cover the same doctrine. To properly understand baptism, one must look at every passage that refers to baptism and try to understand the context of each one.

Once you understand the context of each passage you must now put all the passages together to understand the full meaning of the doctrine. Another example would be Exodus 23:26. Here it is clear that if someone follows God's law, God will fulfill the "number of [His] days." How do we know what the number of his days are, though? A search of the Scripture will provide the answer. In Psalm 90:10, the Psalmist says, "The days of our years are threescore years and ten; and if by reason of strength they be fourscore years" (seventy years or eighty years if you are strong). It can now be determined that practicing God's law will give seventy years of life.

Any doctrine of Scripture is understandable if we, "Study to show [ourselves] approved unto God." This is how a lawyer would study law and is referred to as code pleading in modern law. It is important to code plead the Scripture to understand it. Code pleading is a "statutory scheme that required a plaintiff to plead sufficient facts to give rise to a claim for relief."[14] Code pleading is a simplified form of the ancient Common Law pleading. It is the method one uses to bring facts and evidence before a court of law. As said before, believers need to study the Scripture as a law book just like a lawyer would study the law to prepare for trial. This type of study could take some time and effort, which is why it makes believers "approved unto God." God wrote the Scripture like a law book, line upon line, precept upon precept, here a little and there a little, and this is a perfect description of legal code. The Scripture can be better understood by this type of study.

------

[14] "Code Pleading Legal Definition." Quimbee, www.quimbee.com/keyterms/code-pleading. Accessed 1 July 2020.

This type of study is what is missing in churches today. Believers often point out how an atheist takes verses out of context, but the truth is believers do the same thing when studying biblical doctrines. Looking to our court system when citing a previous court case as evidence, the judge will determine if the evidence is on point and in context. If the evidence is off point or out of context the evidence will be dismissed. The same is to be true when studying the Scripture. Many times, people quote verses off point or out of context to make their point. This is a common error in biblical study. A great example is the study of the resurrection in the Scripture. Many use the story of the rich man and Lazarus to develop a doctrine of the resurrection. If the main point of a specific Scripture is not about the resurrection, then that verse should never be used to study the resurrection. The point to the rich man and Lazarus is not to explain the resurrection, but rather to show that, "If they hear not Moses and the prophets, neither will they be persuaded, though one rose from the dead" (Luke 16:31). This verse is not describing the resurrection and has not met the evidentiary standards to be admitted into evidence for the resurrection. It is taken off point and out of context. The resurrection, however, is thoroughly explained in 1 Corinthians 15. This chapter would be admitted into evidence when studying the resurrection. It is important to have these same high standards when studying the Scripture as when bringing evidence to trial in today's court system.

Another example of this is how modern laws provide definitions of words. When reading a statute, often the definition of words might not be clear. The definition to that word is usually provided in a certain place within the statute, usually near the beginning. You cannot understand the statute until you understand the meaning of the word as defined by the statute. The Scripture is the same. For example, throughout the Scripture the word sin is used, but many times this word is misunderstood. Looking up the word in a Hebrew or Greek Dictionary is a good start, but even this does not provide the scriptural definition of sin. According to James Strong and his concise dictionary of the Greek and Hebrew words of the Bible, sin is, "to miss the mark; to sin." [15] [16] This definition, nonetheless, is incomplete. The question needs to be asked, what mark is missed? If we search the Scripture we will find that God provided a definition for us to use. In 1 John 3:4 the apostle writes, "Whoever commits sin transgresses also the law: **for sin is the transgression of the law**" (1 John 3:4). The scriptural definition of sin is the transgression of God's law. The mark missed is the Law of God. This is the definition that should be used for the word sin in the Scripture. Another example of this is the word love (agape). The definition of love (agape) in the Scripture comes from 1 John 5:2-3. Here the Apostle John says, "By this we know that we love the children of God, when we love God, and keep his commandments. For this is the love of God, **that we keep his commandments**" (1 John 5:2-3). Whenever the word love is translated from the Greek word agape, the definition is "keeping his commandments." Understanding the definition of key

---

[15] Strong, James, "Sin – ἁμαρτάνω - hamartanō." *A Concise Dictionary of the Words in the Greek Bible*, pg. 10, G264.

[16] Strong, James, "Sin – חָטָא - châṭâ'." *A Concise Dictionary of the Words in the Hebrew Bible*, pg. 38, H2398.

words in the Scripture is of vital importance when studying and it is imperative that the definition God provided in the Scripture is the one used even when it might contradict a Hebrew or Greek dictionary.

This is the basics of biblical interpretation. Once the Bible is looked at as a law book and that it is written in legal code, code pleading the Scripture will get the correct understanding. However, with all this said, there is still one more point that must be considered. In Psalm 111:10 the psalmist states, "The fear of YHVH is the beginning of wisdom: **a good understanding have all they that do his commandments**: his praise endures forever." To understand the word of God obedience to His Law is necessary. This is what James meant when he said, "Be ye doers of the word, and not hearers only, deceiving your own selves" (James 1:22). Deception is the opposite of understanding. James continues by saying, "For if any be a hearer of the word, and not a doer, he is like unto a man beholding his natural face in a glass: For he beholds himself, and goes his way, and straightway forgets what manner of man he was. **But whoso looks into the perfect law of liberty, and continues therein**, he being not a forgetful hearer, but a doer of the work, this man shall be blessed in his deed" (James 1:23-25). His point is to look into the Law of God and judge yourself. Not doing the word, or God's law, will lead to deception. Man cannot understand something until he has practical experience with it. It is worth repeating, as Psalms 111:10 says, "The fear of YHVH is the beginning of wisdom: **a good understanding have all they that do his commandments**: his praise endures forever." The only way to understand God's law is to "do his commandments." All the study in the world might help, but to truly understand God's word through His eyes it is important to study with obedience. This writer can attest to this. In 2008, this writer and his family decided to start practicing as many of God's commandments as possible. As more and more commandments were practiced, greater and greater understanding came. It is now very clear why God gave His law. Each law has a benefit received here and now. This writer would encourage everyone to give this a try and see if God was right all along when He gave His law. Start with the "least commandments" (Matt. 5:19) like keeping the Holy Days (Lev. 23) or putting the Ten Commandments on your gate and front door (Deut. 6:9). As one starts with these, "least" commandments one will eventually start understanding how to apply more and more of God's laws to their lives. It might just lead to a blessed life of God and a greater understanding of the Holy Scripture.

The Spirit vs Letter of the Law:

Though the Scripture is to be studied as a law book, it is important to still understand God's law by His spirit. The word spirit can be misleading, though. Churches today often use this term in the context of the Holy Spirit or a spiritual being. However, this is not the only context where the word spirit is used. In modern law, the word spirit is also used. This is known as the spirit of the law and is often compared to the letter of the law. The spirit vs letter of the law is an idiomatic antithesis. The contrast between the spirit of the law and the letter of the law is found in both modern law and even within the Scriptures. These two terms denote two different interpretive models for law as well as for the Scripture. It is this writer's contention that the scriptural definition of the spirit of the law and the letter of the law is the same as the modern legal definition. This section will take a deeper look at the dichotomy between these two interpretation methods.

The letter of the law is simple to understand. The letter of the law is an interpretation model that strictly adheres to the literal wording used in the specific statute. All that is required to interpret a statute using the letter of the law is to define the words and read the statute as is. Here are a few definitions to consider.

> The *Random House Unabridged Dictionary*: The letter of the law is "the precise wording rather than the spirit or intent."[17]

> The *Cambridge Online Dictionary*: The letter of the law is "the exact words of the law and not its more important general meaning."[18]

> *Webster's Online Dictionary*: The letter of the law is "exactly what the law says."[19]

These definitions make it pretty clear. The letter of the law is the law as written, nothing more and nothing less. At first glance this sounds good; however, there are several problems that can arise from this interpretation model. For example, over time many things change within a nation such as definitions and culture. Both of these can

---

[17] "Letter of the law". *Random House Unabridged Dictionary*, https://www.dictionary.com/browse/letter-of-the-law, Accessed 20 July 2023.

[18] "Letter of the law". *Cambridge Advanced Learner's Dictionary & Thesaurus* © Cambridge University Press, Accessed 20 July 2023.

[19] "The letter of the law." Merriam-Webster.com Dictionary, Merriam-Webster, https://www.merriam-webster.com/dictionary/theletterofthelaw, Accessed 14 June 2020.

modify an interpretation of some statutes. This is a problem that many nations, including the United States, have to deal with when interpreting their founding documents, and this is precisely the problem the Apostle Paul was dealing with when he brought up the spirit of the law. The Apostle Paul even contrasted the spirit with the letter of the law when he said, "But now we are delivered from the law, that being dead wherein we were held; that we should serve in newness of spirit, and not in the oldness of the letter" (Rom. 7:6). It is important to understand this contrast in both modern law and the Scripture as well.

The scriptural understanding of the spirit of the law is more difficult to understand. The spirit of the law is a term used to describe how one is to view the law of the Scripture. However, today this term is very misinterpreted. Many will say, "I practice the law in spirit, not in letter." By saying this, they mean that they do not practice the Law of God at all, but rather, they believe that since the Messiah practiced it for them they no longer need to obey God's commands. This belief could not be further from the truth. The point Paul is making is to define how the Law of God should be interpreted and practiced. Today, however, this term is used to demonstrate that the Law of God is no longer needed. These are two very different understandings. It is very important to discover the true meaning of these two phrases, the spirit of the law and the letter of the law.

The spirit of the law is not a new term. It goes back to ancient times. It is also not simply a biblical term, but has its root in secular law as well. In fact, this principle is still practiced in U.S. law today. This term is used in construing

Constitutional Law, court room policies and procedures, and even the rules of sport and games. The popular poet and playwright, William Shakespeare, dealt with the concepts of spirit of the law vs. letter of the law in some of his plays. Shakespeare's play *The Merchant of Venice* is a perfect example of this. The spirit of the law is not only a biblical phrase but also a secular phrase as well. The question to ask is this, what does the term spirit of the law mean?

Determining the intention of the legislature is the primary rule in construing law. Under most circumstances, the law should be written so as to be clearly understood. Conversely, if a law is determined to be vague and ambiguous, the Canons of Construction will be applied. The Canons of Constructions are a list of basic rules and maxims for interpreting law. A maxim of law is "a rule or principle of law universally admitted, as being just and consonant with reason."[20] These maxims of law are designed to determine the intent of the legislature, which is the primary rule of construing law. Some examples of maxims are listed in Table 2 below.

United States Maxims of Law
• A l'impossible nul n'est tenu - No one is bound to do what is impossible.
• Animus ad se omne jus ducit - It is to the intention that all law applies.
• Expressio unius est exclusio alterius - Whatever is omitted is understood to be excluded.

Table 2

These are just a few of the many maxims of law used to construe statutes with the primary rule to determine

---

[20] Bouvier, John, "Maxim." *A Law Dictionary Adapted to the Constitution and Laws of the United States of America*, Vol. II, pg. 105.

the intent of the legislature. This is what the spirit of the law means in secular law. To confirm this, here are a few legal definitions.

> Webster's Online Dictionary: "the spirit of the law is the aim or **purpose of a law** when it was written."[21]

> US Legal: "Spirit of the law refers to ideas that the creators of a particular law wanted to have effect. It is the **intent and purpose of the lawmaker**."[22]

> *Black's Law Dictionary*: The spirit of the law, "as opposed to the letter of the law, this refers to the meaning and **intent of the law** and those who created the law and what they intended to accomplish in the creation of the law."[23]

From these definitions it is clear, that the spirit of the law, in secular law, is the process by which one determines the intent of the legislature. This is seeking out the true meaning of a law based on what the writers of that law meant. Here is the million-dollar question, what does this have to do with the scriptural definition of the spirit of the law? The answer is simple, they are one and the same definition. Man is to seek out what God intended behind His law. The spirit of the law in the Scripture comes from a couple of verses. In Romans 7:6, the Apostle Paul states, "But now we are delivered from the law, that being dead wherein we were held; that we should serve in newness of

---

[21] "The spirit of the law." Merriam-Webster.com Dictionary, Merriam-Webster, https://www.merriam-webster.com/dictionary/thespiritofthelaw, Accessed 14 June 2020.

[22] "Spirit of the law." USLegal.com, https://definitions.uslegal.com/s/spirit-of-the-law/, Accessed June 3, 2016

[23] "Spirit of the law." Thelaw.com Dictionary (Black's Law Dictionary, 2nd Ed.), https://dictionary.thelaw.com/spirit-of-the-law, Accessed 14 June 2020.

spirit, and not in the oldness of the letter." The comparison between the letter and spirit clearly signifies an interpretive understanding. When Paul says, "we are delivered from the law" he is referring to the "oldness of the letter" of the law. This letter of the law kept them "dead wherein [they] were held." Serving in the "newness of spirit" is a different interpretation of the law. Paul is saying that believers should serve, or submit to, the law in spirit and not the law by the letter. A modern example of this are speed laws. It is common to have a sixty-five mile per hour speed limit. Many times, traffic is traveling seventy-five miles per hour. By the letter of the law a ticket should be given to each driver, but by the spirit of the law a ticket is not given because the law is intended to keep people safe. Traveling too slow for traffic can be dangerous as well. As long as traffic is safe, going slightly beyond the speed limit is okay. In the case of an emergency, such as an injured child, the police officer will often help break the speed laws with an ambulance, flashing lights, and a siren. This is yet another example of how the spirit of the law works. Man is to use their common sense to understand the intent behind God's laws just like they do with man's laws. This is designating how one should interpret God's law. After all, the Pharisees interpreted the Scripture using a very literal "letter" of the law interpretation. In fact, the Pharisees went beyond the letter of the law in their interpretation. Often, they added commandments in order to make sure that God's law was not broken. They did this in an attempt to keep people away from sin. These added laws were called "fence laws." In the Talmud, which contains the writings of the Pharisees, it says,

> Moses received the Law from Sinai and handed it down to Joshua, and Joshua to the elders, and the elders to the prophets, and the prophets handed it down to the men of the Great Assembly. They said three things: Be deliberate in judgment, raise up many disciples, and **make a fence round the Law**.[24]

These fence laws are what the Scripture calls the "tradition of the elders" (Mark 7:3). The tradition of the elders caused the Messiah an enormous amount of problems throughout the Gospels. According to the Messiah, these traditions "made the commandment of God of none effect" (Matt. 15:6). Adding extra laws, even for the purpose of keeping from sin, only diminishes the Law of God. If God's law is truly "the perfect law of liberty" (James 1:25), then adding extra laws will only hinder that liberty. If any law was a burden to the people, it was these added fence laws from the Pharisees. This opens the door for an interpretation that is off point and out of context. Construing law using the letter of the law will many times lead to a legalistic interpretation that completely ignores the true intent of God for that law. When the Apostle Paul was teaching a spiritual interpretation of the law, he was not removing the law, but providing an interpretive model for believers to use in understanding God's law. The spirit of the law from the Scripture's perspective is just like the spirit of the law in the secular world. Believers need to understand God's law with God's intent and purpose in mind.

To understand this better it is necessary to study the Greek and Hebrew words used for spirit in the Scripture.

---

[24] Pirke Avoth, Chapter 1, Mishnah 1

The Hebrew word for spirit is רוּחַ (ruach). This word speaks of the breath of God. Strong's Dictionary defines it as, "wind; by resemblance breath, that is, a sensible (or even violent) exhalation."[25] The Greek word for spirit is πνεῦμα (pneuma), which means, "a current of air, that is, breath (blast) or a breeze."[26] Both the Greek and Hebrew word for spirit references the breath of God. In light of our current legal definition for the spirit of the law, these two words demonstrate that the scriptural definition of the spirit of the law is the same. A person's breath represents their spoken word. What people say represents their purpose, their drive, or their intent. When studying God's law, it is imperative to understand it by God's breath, or His purpose, His drive, and His intent. The goal is to determine the intent and purpose God had for that law. After all, God is the lawmaker of the Scripture and it is His interpretation (breath/spirit) that believers need to understand. In fact, this phrase is used in many similar ways today. For example, someone might say, "In the spirit of cooperation, let's put aside our differences." They also might say, "In the spirit of fairness, we all need to obey the rules." They also might say, "In the spirit of Mother Theresa, let us feed the hungry." This shows the word spirit as meaning to follow the example and understanding of a person or concept. This is how the Scripture is to be interpreted, in the Spirit of YHVH, or the spirit of His law.

This is what the Apostle Paul meant when he said, "All Scripture is given by inspiration of God" (2 Tim. 3:16). The

---

[25] Strong, James, "Spirit – רוּחַ - rûach." *A Concise Dictionary of the Words in the Hebrew Bible*, pg. 107, H7307.

[26] Strong, James, "Spirit – πνεῦμα - pneuma." *A Concise Dictionary of the Words in the Greek Bible*, pg. 107, G4151.

word for "inspiration of God" is θεόπνευστος (theopneustos), which literally means "divinely breathed in."[27] This word is a combination of theos, which refers to God and pneuma which is the word for spirit or breath. Paul is saying that the Scripture is God-breathed. This is what the Apostle Peter meant when he said, "Knowing this first, that no prophecy of the Scripture is of any private interpretation. For the prophecy came not in old time by the will of man: but holy men of God spoke as they were moved by the Holy Spirit" (2 Pet. 1:20-21). This is the definition of the spirit of the law. Believers are not to interpret the Scripture at all, but instead they are to study the Scripture by searching out every reference to a concept until they understand the Scripture the way God intended. Keep in mind, this does not provide the liberty to "wrest [the] Scriptures", for this will only bring their "own destruction" (2 Pet. 3:15-16). Believers need to be diligent to study the Scripture the way God instructed with the goal to determine His intent and purpose.

To summarize, the Bible is a law book, written in legal code. Isaiah 28:9-14 states so. As Isaiah said, "For precept must be upon precept, precept upon precept; line upon line, line upon line; here a little, and there a little" (Is. 28:10). Believers need to read each verse pertaining to each subject and understand the immediate context of the verse, which is what Isaiah means by "precept upon precept; line upon line." Then believers need to take every verse on the subject and put them together, which is what

---

[27] Strong, James, "Inspiration of God – θεόπνευστος - theopneustos." *A Concise Dictionary of the Words in the Greek Bible*, pg. 107, G2315.

Isaiah means by "here a little, and there a little." However, each verse taken needs to be on point and in context. This means each verse used is directly about the topic being studied. No study based on inference would be allowed. This method of study is what a lawyer would call code pleading.   It comes from the ancient Common Law pleading. It is how a lawyer studies law to prepare for trial. When studying the Scripture with this method, seeking God's intent and purpose, the Scripture quickly becomes clear.

The Scripture is not without interpretive examples. Many times, God provided examples to learn from (1 Cor. 10:11). In fact, this is how law works. God's law includes several hundred commandments, statutes and judgments. Commandments represent the basic laws of the Scripture. Statutes are specific laws to explain a specific command. Judgments are examples of how to construe/interpret specific commandments and statutes. It is with these judgments that we can see an example of how God intended us to study the Scripture. Here are a few examples of judgments in the Scripture:

The Building of the Temple:

The Temple was built by King Solomon around the 10th century BC. This Temple was similar to the Tabernacle, but was quite different in many ways. For example, the Tabernacle was mobile and built like a tent (Ex. 35:10-11). The Temple was not mobile and was built out of stone (1 Kings 6:7). There were several other differences as well, but the question to ask is this, why was King Solomon allowed to break the specific commands of how to build the Tabernacle (Ex. 25:8-9)? This is an example of the spirit of the law. God's intent for the Tabernacle was to be used as a legal system while in the wilderness (this will be discussed more in book two). They were a nomadic society that moved often. A mobile tent is exactly what Israel needed at this time. During Solomon's reign, Israel was settled in the land and so building a permanent structure was within the spirit of the law. Both the Tabernacle and the Temple served the same purpose for the nation even though they were different.

David Eating the Showbread:

In 1 Samuel 21:3-6 King David was hungry and needed some bread. He asked the priest for bread, but only the showbread from the Temple was available. This bread was forbidden by God's law for anyone to eat except the priests, yet David broke this law and ate it anyway (Lev. 24:5-9). It is true that David broke the letter of the law, but he did not break the spirit of the law. The Messiah explains this in Matt. 12:3-4. The Messiah said, "Have you not read what David did, when he was hungry, and they that were with him; how he entered into the house of God, and did eat the showbread, which was not lawful for him to eat, neither for them which were with him, but only for the priests?" (Matt. 12:3-4). The intent of the law concerning the showbread was not to cause someone to starve, which made it okay for David to eat. Nevertheless, it would be sin if David made a practice of this and ate the showbread on normal occasions (Heb. 10:26).

Ox in the Ditch:

When the Messiah dealt with the Pharisees regarding working on the Sabbath, one of his examples was that of a man leading his ox to drink water, or a man freeing his ox stuck in a ditch (Luke 13:15, 14:5). These are examples of using the spirit of the law to interpret the Law of God. God's intent for the Sabbath was not for an animal to go thirsty, or for an animal to die in a ditch so we could rest. It is okay to deal with basic animal needs on the Sabbath when necessary. However, it would be against the Sabbath laws to intentionally do unnecessary work on the Sabbath, even work regarding the care of animals. We cannot use the spirit of the law as an excuse to break the Sabbath, but when a need arises the grace to break the letter of the law is available.

Do Not Muzzle an Ox:

In 1 Corinthians 9:7-9, the Apostle Paul uses the spirit of the law to explain a scriptural principle. The law for not muzzling an ox while he is working is to allow the working animal to eat and provide the needed energy to complete the work. It is wrong to keep the ox from keeping up its strength. Likewise, you can extract from this law that man can eat of the fruit of his labors as well. The fact that this law can be used to explain a principle that governs man does not remove the fact that it still governs the ox. This verse does not give a new explanation of the law for muzzling an ox, but further explains the intent of God for this law. It applies to humans and animals alike.

<u>Sabbath Laws:</u>

There are two laws regarding the Sabbath that need to be interpreted using the spirit of the law. One law says you are not to travel on the Sabbath (Ex. 16:29). How is this law to be interpreted? Since another commandment also says not to forsake the assembly on the Sabbath (Lev. 23:3, Heb. 10:25), it can be concluded that there is an exception to travel to the Sabbath assembly. There might also be other emergencies that would allow for the breaking of the letter of this law as well. Another law says you cannot kindle a fire on the Sabbath (Ex. 35:3). Since this statute was in regards to working on the Sabbath, it can be concluded that warming your house on the Sabbath during cold temperatures is okay, but if you use fire in your occupation, such as a blacksmith, then you cannot kindle a fire for work. Fire used to heat your home is not work, but fire used to shape metal for an occupation is work.

These are just a few examples of how to interpret God's law using the spirit of the law. Believers are to interpret His commandments based upon His intended purpose. This is what Isaiah meant when he said the Messiah would "magnify the law and make it honorable" (Isaiah 42:21). The Messiah came and demonstrated how to properly understand God's law. This in no way removes the letter of the law because the Messiah clearly used the letter of the law as well. In Matthew 5:17-19, the Messiah mentions the importance of every "jot" and "tittle" of God's law. An example of how the Messiah interpreted the Scripture is in explaining the resurrection. The Sadducees questioned the Messiah about the resurrection. His answer was simple, yet he interpreted the Scripture by the letter of the Law. His answer was, "Have you not read in the book of Moses, how in the bush God spoke unto him, saying, I am the God of Abraham, and the God of Isaac, and the God of Jacob? He is not the God of the dead, but the God of the living: you therefore do greatly error" (Mark 12:26-27). The Messiah used the tense of a verb to properly understand the resurrection. This is very literal and a good demonstration of the letter of the law and its proper use. If the letter of the law fits with the spirit of the law, then a very literal letter of the law interpretation is warranted.

Sometimes, however, the letter of the law does not apply for today. A great example of this is the law to put a rail around the roof of your house (Deut. 22:8). This commandment made perfect sense for the time it was written. They had flat roofs that had rails because it was their patio and was often used for entertaining. A rail was necessary for safety. Today, most homes have pitched roofs and no one spends time on the roof. There is no reason to have a rail around a pitched roof, but a balcony that is used for people to stand on should require a rail. Guess what, America does have a law that requires any balcony over thirty inches high must have a rail on it. America does not follow the letter of this law, but they do follow the spirit of this law.

The spirit of the law has always been the way God intended the Scripture to be interpreted. This does not mean one can ignore the letter of the law, but it does mean one needs to make sure the letter of the law fits with the spirit of the law (God's intended purpose), when judgments are made. This concept is what the Pharisees lacked in their own understanding of God's law. They took this to an extreme and continually added extra commands to God's law to make sure the people followed the letter of the law. The Messiah dealt with this many times in His encounters with the Pharisees. He was constantly accused of breaking God's law (Matt. 15:1-9, Mark 7:5-8). The truth is the Messiah never once broke God's law. If He did He could not have been the Messiah. The fact is, the Messiah was accused of breaking the "tradition of the elders" (Matt. 15:2) and not the Law of God. God's people need to study God's law using biblical principles of study. The intent of their study should be to find out how God Himself intended the law to be. After all, this is what the spirit of the law means. It is the intent of the lawmaker that is the law.

The Mission of Israel:

Now that there is a good understanding of how to interpret God's law, it is important to understand the context of how God gave His law. On Mount Sinai God gave His Law to Moses and the children of Israel. Please remember that this was just the codification of God's law. This is not the beginning of God's law. God's law is eternal. In fact, God's law is said to be forever hundreds of times in the Scripture (Ex. 12:14, Ex. 12:17, Ex. 12:24, Ex. 17:21, Ex. 28:43, Ex. 29:28, Ex. 30:21, Ex. 31:17, Ex. 32:13, Lev. 6:18, Lev. 6:22, Lev. 7:34, Lev. 7:36, Lev. 10:9, Lev. 10:15, Lev. 16:29, Lev. 16:31, Lev. 23:14, Lev. 23:21, Lev. 23:41, Lev. 24:3, Lev. 25:23, Lev. 25:46, Num. 10:8, Num. 15:15, Num. 18:8, Num. 18:11, Num. 18:19, Num. 18:23, Num. 19:10, Deut. 4:40, Deut. 18:5, Deut. 19:9, Deut. 23:3, Deut. 28:46, just to name a few). God's law was not for Israel only. Foreigners were required to keep His Law as well. The Scripture declares that "one law shall be to him that is home born, and unto the stranger that sojourns among you" (Ex. 12:49). Israel and foreigners alike were to keep God's commandments. In fact, God punished Sodom (Gen. 13:13), Gomorrah (Gen. 13:10), the Amorites (Gen. 15:16) and Nineveh (Jonah 1:1-2) for breaking His Law. These are all non-Israelite nations. This is hardly fair for God to judge a nation for breaking a law they were not required to follow.

The truth is that God's law was instituted well before Moses on Mount Sinai. God's law was in the Garden of Eden. The Apostle Paul said, "where no law is, there is no transgression" (Rom. 4:15). Adam could not have sinned if there was no law. The Sabbath law was instituted on day seven of creation when God "blessed the seventh day and sanctified it" (Gen. 2:3). This was very early in the history of man. Noah understood God's law as well. He understood clean and unclean meats. How else could God have commanded Noah to take seven of "every clean beast" unless Noah understood the clean and unclean statutes (Gen. 7:2)? Noah even understood the sacrificial system, which is the topic of the second book of this series, when he "built an altar unto YHVH" and "offered burnt offerings on the altar" (Gen. 8:20). Even the Patriarch Abraham practiced God's law. The Scripture declares that Abraham "obeyed my voice, and kept my charge, my commandments, my statutes, and my laws" (Gen. 26:5). How else could Abraham have practiced all of God's law, including "His commandments, statutes, and laws?" These are clear evidence that God's law was known before

Mount Sinai. Remember, just because all laws were not mentioned, does not mean that all laws were not known. All of God's law existed before creation because God's law is a mirror of Himself. Here are some descriptions of God that are also used of His Law. They are both called: good (Luke 18:19, Rom. 7:12), holy (Is. 5:16, Rom. 7:12), just (Deut. 32:4, Rom. 7:12), truth (Deut. 32:4, Ps. 119:143, 151), perfect (Matt. 5:48, Ps. 19:7), without burden (Matt. 11:30, 1 John 5:3), love (1 John 4:8, Rom. 13:10), righteous (Ex. 9:27, Ps. 19:8), spiritual (John 4:24, Rom. 7:14), unchangeable (Mal. 3:6, Matt. 5:18), and eternal (Gen. 21:33, Ps. 111:7-8). *See table 3.*

A Comparison of God and His Law		
Quality	God	Law
Good	Luke 18:19	Rom. 7:12
Holy	Isaiah 5:16	Romans 7:12
Just	Deuteronomy 32:4	Romans 7:12
Truth	Deuteronomy 32:4	Psalms 119:43, 151
Perfect	Matthew 5:48	Psalms 19:7
Without burden	Matthew 11:30	1 John 5:3
Love	1 John 4:8	Romans 13:10
Righteous	Exodus 9:27	Psalms 19:8
Spiritual	John 4:24	Romans 7:14
Unchangeable	Malachi 3:6	Matthew 5:18
Eternal	Genesis 21:33	Psalms 111:7-8

Table 3

God's law is a picture of who He is and all peoples and nations are expected to maintain that picture. After all, mankind was created in the image of God (Gen. 1:27). The expectation is that mankind will maintain that same image. God still holds all people and nations accountable to His Law. In fact, by the end of this book it will be clear that the rise and fall of every nation is based on their obedience to that Law. This is why the Apostle Paul said, "What advantage then has the Jew? Or what profit is there of circumcision? Much in every way: chiefly, because that unto them were committed the oracles of God" (Rom. 3:1-2). The advantage of being a Jew is that God gave them His oracles written down containing His law, history, and prophets. This was a huge advantage over every other nation. The other nations had to glean from Israel to learn the Law of God. Today this is no longer true. God's oracles are written down in His word and are readily available for almost any who desires them.

How God's law was known prior to the Mosaic Codification is unclear. Remember, codification is a systematic "process of compiling rules and laws into an orderly, formal code."[28] Some have speculated that it might have been written in the stars. Others suggest it was handed down verbally from generation to generation. It is not the intent of this book to try and answer this question. What is clear is that mankind knew the Law of God from the very beginning. At the time of Moses, God decided to call out a nation for His purposes. It is here where God spelled out His Law and codified it for the nation of Israel. This purpose was for Israel to be an example for all nations to follow. Through Israel God would bless the nations. When God called Abram He said, "In thee shall all families of the earth be blessed" (Gen. 12:3). When Solomon prayed during the dedication of the Temple he said;

> Hear you in heaven your dwelling place, and do according to all that the stranger calls to you for: that all people of the earth may know your name, to fear you, as do your people Israel; and that they

---

[28] Wex Definitions Team, Wex Legal Information Institute, Cornell Law School, "Codification." August of 2022, obtained July, 28, 2024, https://www.law.cornell.edu/wex/codification

> may know that this house, which I have built, is called by your name. (1 Kings 8:43)

The Apostle Paul put it this way.

> Behold, you are called a Jew, and rest in the law, and make your boast of God, and know his will, and approve the things that are more excellent, being instructed out of the law; and are confident that you are **a guide of the blind, a light of them which are in darkness, an instructor of the foolish, a teacher of babes**, which have the form of knowledge and of the truth in the law. You therefore which teach another, you teach not yourself? You that preach a man should not steal, do you steal? (Rom. 2:17-21).

Israel was to be a guide of the blind, a light to them in darkness, an instructor of the foolish and a teacher of babes. They were to be an example to all nations.

Israel's purpose was to bring God's law to the nations. Unfortunately, they failed their mission, but fortunately for us, the Messiah did not fail this mission. He started it, and the apostles were appointed to continue it, going to every nation. The Messiah's purpose was to die a sacrificial death for the forgiveness of sins. The Apostle Paul said, "In whom we have redemption through his blood, even the forgiveness of sins:" (Col. 1:14). The Messiah did this by keeping every commandment of God, thus fulfilling the law (Matt. 5:17). This in no way removed God's law, but rather endorses it. The purpose of the Messiah was not to destroy the law, but to "magnify the law, and make it honorable" (Is. 42:21). The Messiah died for our sins to bring man back to God and keep His commandments.

These are the same commandments that were codified by Moses on Mount Sinai. These commandments are eternal and are an example of the very character of God.

The Mosaic Codification:

By the time Moses enters the scene God decided to codify His Law for mankind. He chose to do this through Moses and the nation of Israel. It has already been demonstrated that the Bible is a law book and is written in legal code. This law is a national law to govern nations. Using the principles of study mentioned earlier, if the Law of God was to be organized, or codified, it would be organized under two commandments. The Messiah was asked, "Which is the great commandment in the law?" To which the Messiah responded,

> You shall love YHVH your God with all your heart, and with all your soul, and with all your mind. This is the first and great commandment. And the second is like unto it, you shall love your neighbor as yourself. **On these two commandments hang all the law and the prophets**. (Matt. 22:36-40).

All of God's law fits under these two commandments. First come the Ten Commandments. The first five commandments fit under, "Love YHVH your God" and the last five commandments fit under, "Love your neighbor as yourself." The rest of the statutes and judgments of God fit under each one of the Ten Commandments. On the next page is a chart to help demonstrate this. This chart is also available in a larger format at the beginning of this book on page xii.

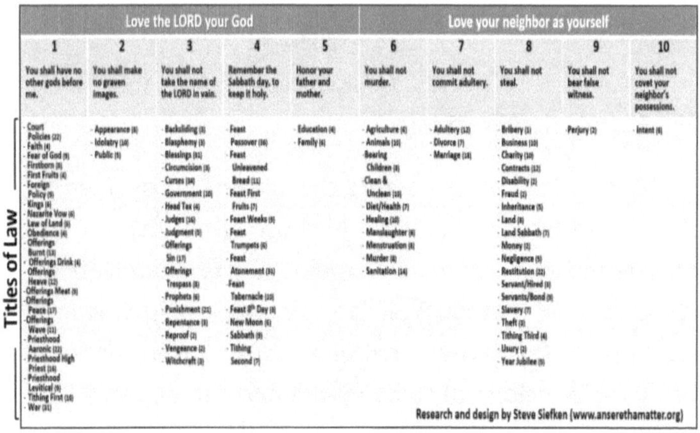

Love the LORD your God					Love your neighbor as yourself				
1	**2**	**3**	**4**	**5**	**6**	**7**	**8**	**9**	**10**
You shall have no other gods before me.	You shall make no graven images.	You shall not take the name of the LORD in vain.	Remember the Sabbath day, to keep it holy.	Honor your father and mother.	You shall not murder.	You shall not commit adultery.	You shall not steal.	You shall not bear false witness.	You shall not covet your neighbor's possessions.
- Court Policies (22) - Faith (4) - Fear of God (9) - Firstborn (8) - First Fruits (4) - Foreign Policy (9) - Kings (6) - Nazarite Vow (6) - Law of Land (5) - Obedience (4) - Offerings Burnt (13) - Offerings Drink (4) - Offerings Heave (12) - Offerings Meat (9) - Offerings Peace (17) - Offerings Wave (11) - Priesthood Aaronic (22) - Priesthood High Priest (16) - Priesthood Levitical (9) - Tithing First (16) - War (31)	- Appearance (8) - Idolatry (14) - Public (9)	- Backsliding (3) - Blasphemy (3) - Blessings (31) - Circumcision (3) - Curses (34) - Government (28) - Head Tax (4) - Judges (14) - Judgment (3) - Offerings Sin (17) - Offerings Trespass (8) - Prophets (6) - Punishment (21) - Repentance (3) - Reproof (2) - Vengeance (2) - Witchcraft (3)	- Feast Passover (36) - Feast Unleavened Bread (11) - Feast First Fruits (7) - Feast Weeks (9) - Feast Trumpets (6) - Feast Atonement (34) - Feast Tabernacle (10) - Feast 8th Day (8) - New Moon (6) - Sabbath (9) - Tithing Second (7)	- Education (4) - Family (6)	- Agriculture (6) - Animals (10) -Bearing Children (8) -Clean & Unclean (18) - Diet/Health (7) - Healing (10) - Manslaughter (6) - Menstruation (8) - Murder (8) - Sanitation (14)	- Adultery (12) - Divorce (7) - Marriage (14)	- Bribery (1) - Business (10) - Charity (10) - Contracts (12) - Disability (2) - Fraud (2) - Inheritance (5) - Land (8) - Land Sabbath (7) - Money (2) - Negligence (5) - Restitution (22) - Servant/Hired (8) - Servants/Bond (9) - Slavery (7) - Theft (3) - Tithing Third (4) - Usury (2) - Year Jubilee (9)	- Perjury (2)	- Intent (6)

Research and design by Steve Siefken (www.anserethamatter.org)

An example of the Mosaic Law codified as the Messiah described. Created by author. Larger version on page xii.

The above example is the work of this writer. It was developed from 2008 until the writing of this book. The Mosaic Law contains 757 commandments, statutes, and judgments. These are all codified, or organized, into eighty-eight titles of law. These titles are represented in the bottom row of this chart. The titles are listed with the number of statutes under each title. These eighty-eight titles of law fall under one or more of the Ten Commandments, which hang on the two great commandments to Love YHVH your God and love your neighbor as yourself. Of course, this model is only an example of the description provided by the Messiah himself. In no way should anyone be emphatic regarding the specifics in this chart. In fact, the numbers given only serve as an example. Many statutes could easily be divided into two or even three statutes. Likewise, groups of statutes could easily be combined into one statute as well. It is not the purpose of this book to argue for a specific number. The Jews counted the Mosaic Law and came up with six hundred and thirteen. This is the same law but a different count. The purpose here is to demonstrate how to study the Mosaic Law. It is a law and needs to be studied as law. Studying the law in this manner will provide many reasons why nations should practice God's law today.

The question to ask is this, where does God's law fit in with biblical salvation? This is the question that has been overlooked for quite some time. In fact, the answer to this question will settle this entire debate.

Chapter Three

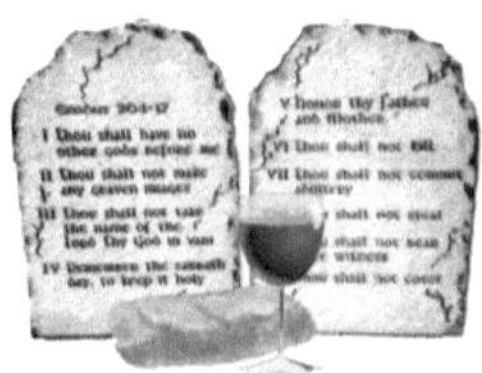

What is Salvation?

One of the more difficult concepts to accept regarding God's law is just how it fits into God's plan of salvation. This can sometimes be a tough hill to climb. Messianic believers and Christians who follow the Torah have to wrestle with this. Often, this is difficult to overcome because churches have engrained into believers for quite some time the idea that God's law is the antithesis of grace. Believers today have been taught that grace and law are mutually exclusive. This is a very unfortunate reality, but is easily overcome with a good biblical understanding of salvation. Once the Torah is put into the right place within salvation, all of the problems disappear. Here is a quick overview of the salvation process expounded in the Scripture. There are three aspects to salvation: justification (Rom. 4:25), sanctification (1 Thess. 4:3), and glorification (Rom. 8:30). The understanding of these three doctrines are critical to understanding the place of God's law in the New Covenant. Once these three aspects are properly understood, it will be clear how God's law fits into His plan. The following is a quick overview of each aspect of God's salvation plan.

What is Justification?

The first and primary aspect of God's salvation plan is justification. The word justification δικαίωσις (dikaiōsis), literally means "an acquittal".[29] Man is guilty of a crime (sin - Rom. 3:23) and owes the penalty for sin (death - Rom. 6:23). All men are in the same position before God, which is guilty. God has a standard set forth for man, and it is recorded in His law. This standard is perfection (Matt. 5:48). The standard was missed by breaking God's law, which is what is called sin (1 John 3:4). According to biblical law, in order for one to pay for their crimes (sins) a blood sacrifice would have to be given. As Hebrews 9:22 states, "without shedding of blood is no remission." Man owes a death penalty that he cannot pay.

This is why the Messiah was needed. He had to live the life that man could not. The Messiah obeyed every commandment, statute, and judgement of God (Matt. 5:17-20), yet suffered the penalty for sin in spite of this. This was a penalty he did not deserve, but since he paid this penalty he is now qualified to pay for man's sins. In Hebrew law, the High Priest would enter the holy of holies once a year on the day of atonement. This day was a

---

[29] Strong, James, "Justification - dikaiōsis." *A Concise Dictionary of the Words in the Greek Bible*, pg. 23, G1347.

special day to sacrifice for both the sins of the High Priest and the sins of all the people (Lev. 16:6,15, Heb. 9:7). It was this day that brought atonement for the sins of all the people of God, but only for one year. In Hebrews 9:8, the author speaking of this day writes, "the Holy Ghost this signifying, that the way into the holiest of all was not yet made manifest." The holiest of all is where the presence of God dwells in the Tabernacle. Ancient Hebrews did not understand this special day. They couldn't have. For it was "not yet made manifest." The manifestation was that of the Messiah dying on a cross. The Messiah has now become our high priest to sacrifice on our behalf. The sacrifice made by the Messiah was perfect, for he sacrificed himself. Man can now be acquitted (justified) of their crimes (sins) against God by this sacrifice. The question is, how do they become justified?

The Scripture is not silent on this issue. There are a few things mentioned that are necessary for salvation. A blood sacrifice, repentance, faith, belief, and confession are among those mentioned. The hardest part has already been done by the Messiah. A perfect man was needed to pay the penalty for sin. Thankfully, the Messiah qualified when he provided himself as a worthy sacrifice. Man's part is simple. Man needs to repent, have faith, believe, and confess to be sure he has been justified. The problem is, what do these words mean?

The first thing necessary for justification is repentance, but many do not understand what this word means. The accepted meaning of this word today is "to turn around" or "about face." It was a military term applied to the Scripture. Using this definition would make repentance mean to turn from your sins. This is an unfortunate understanding today because the biblical meaning is quite different. The word translated as repent in the Hebrew Scripture is נָחַם (nâcham), which means "to sigh, ... breathe strongly, ... to be sorry, ... to regret."[30] The Greek word used in the New Testament is μετανοέω (metanoeō), which means "to think differently or afterwards, ... to reconsider, ... to change your mind."[31] This is quite a bit different than today's understanding. It appears that all God expects from us is "to change our mind." But change our minds about what? We will understand this better as we look at the other things necessary for salvation.

The second and third thing necessary for justification will be covered together, for they are really the same thing. Faith and belief have a very similar definition in English as well as Greek and Hebrew. Webster's dictionary defines faith as "allegiance to duty or a person"[32] and belief as "a state or habit of mind in which trust or confidence is placed in some person or thing."[33] These are very good definitions because the Strong's Dictionary definition of πίστις (pistis/faith) and πιστεύω (pisteuō/believe) are the same. Pistis (faith) means a "persuasion, that is, credence; moral conviction"[34] and

---

[30] Strong, James, "Repent – נָחַם (nâcham)." *A Concise Dictionary of the Words in the Hebrew Bible*, pg. 77, H5162.

[31] Strong, James, "Repent – μετανοέω (metanoeō)." *A Concise Dictionary of the Words in the Greek Bible*, pg. 47, H3340.

[32] "Faith." Merriam-Webster.com Dictionary, Merriam-Webster, https://www.merriam-webster.com/dictionary/faith. Accessed 9 Jun. 2024.

[33] "Belief." Merriam-Webster.com Dictionary, Merriam-Webster, https://www.merriam-webster.com/dictionary/belief. Accessed 9 Jun. 2024.

[34] Strong, James, "Faith – πίστις - pistis." *A Concise Dictionary of the Words in the Greek Bible*, pg. 58, G4102.

pisteuō (believe) means "to have faith in ... to entrust."[35] Even in Hebrew, they have the same meaning. The Hebrew word 'êmûn (faith) means "trustworthiness" and the word 'âman (believe) means "faithful, to trust or believe."[36] These words are even spelled similarly in Greek and Hebrew. The meaning could not be clearer. Faith and belief mean to believe something so strongly that you put your trust in it.

The last requirement for justification is confession. The Greek word for confess is ὁμολογέω (homologeō) which means "to assent" or to "acknowledge."[37] This is the extension of faith/belief, which is to really mean it. You can't just say you believe or have faith in the Messiah, you have to really mean it as demonstrated with behavior and actions. The Hebrew word for confess is יָדָה (yâdâh) and comes from the root word yâd which means "to open your hand, indicating power, means, or direction."[38] Confession is a way of simply showing everyone that you really believe it. It is not simply "honoring with your lips," it must be meant with all your heart (Matt. 15:8).

To understand repentance combined with faith/belief/confession you simply need to listen to the words of the Messiah. In Mark 1:15, the Messiah makes the statement, "repent ye, and believe the gospel." If we

---

[35] Strong, James, "Believe – πιστεύω - pisteuō." *A Concise Dictionary of the Words in the Greek Bible*, pg. 58, G4100.

[36] Strong, James, "Faith – אֱמוּן - 'êmûn." *A Concise Dictionary of the Words in the Hebrew Bible*, pg. 14, H529.

[37] Strong, James, "Confess – ὁμολογέω - homologeō." *A Concise Dictionary of the Words in the Greek Bible*, pg. 52, G3670.

[38] Strong, James, "Confess – יָדָה - yâdâh." *A Concise Dictionary of the Words in the Hebrew Bible*, pg. 47, H3034.

understood repentance like the modern definition, this statement would mean, "turn from your sins ye, and believe the gospel." This is very unfortunate because it sure sounds like you have to earn salvation by turning from your sins. This can't be true for, "by grace are you saved through faith; and that not of yourselves: it is the gift of God: not of works, lest any man should boast" (Eph. 2:8-9). Rather, the Messiah is saying to "change your mind" (repent) "and believe the gospel" (death, burial, resurrection 1 Cor. 15:1-4), or, in other words, stop believing whatever was believed before, and start believing that the Messiah died, was buried, and rose again to pay for man's sins. However, as has already been seen, this has to truly be believed. This is something entirely different.

Give this a try: read through the New Testament and understand repent as "changing your mind" and see how well it fits. This is truly the only understanding that allows salvation to be a "free gift" by "grace" alone. The evidence of your belief is your changed life, which the Bible calls sanctification.

What is Sanctification?

The second part of salvation is called sanctification. The word sanctification ἁγιασμός (hagiasmos), literally means "purification" or "consecration" or to be "set apart."[39] This word is always translated as "holiness" or "sanctification." While justification is purely the act of God

---

[39] Strong, James, "Sanctification – ἁγιασμός - hagiasmos." *A Concise Dictionary of the Words in the Greek Bible*, pg. 7, G38.

pardoning the sinner's transgressions, sanctification is the act of God and man consecrating the sinner to the life that God prescribed for us (Phil.2:12-13, Eph. 2:10).

Justification is an instantaneous act where God declares a sinner to be righteous before Him based solely on the sinner's belief (Rom. 4:3). It is not earned by the works of the law (Gal. 2:16), but is a free gift from God (Rom. 6:23). Since salvation is free, does that mean the believer can sin as he pleases? Certainly not, for the Apostle Paul states clearly, "What shall we say then? Shall we continue in sin, that grace may abound? God forbid. How shall we, that are dead to sin, live any longer therein?" (Rom. 6:1-2, 15) After believers have received this free gift, they are no longer to live in sin. The question must be asked, what is sin? The answer is in 1 John 3:4 where the Apostle John states that, "Whosoever commits sin transgresses also the law: for sin is the transgression of the law." Here is the answer. Man sins when he breaks God's law. God offers us forgiveness and a full pardon, but after someone repents and believes the gospel, they have to turn from sin and back to Him. Or, to put it another way, they have to stop breaking His law and start following it. This then is sanctification. It is a lifelong process of turning back to following God's law. It is the maturing of the believer. It is fighting the good fight. Paul said, "Fight the good fight of faith, lay hold on eternal life, whereunto you are also called, and have professed a good profession before many witnesses." (1 Tim. 6:12). The "good fight" that Paul speaks of is the fight of faith. Paul also said, "I have fought a good fight, I have finished my course, I have kept the faith" (2 Tim. 4:7). The goal is not to have faith, but to keep faith for an entire life. This will ultimately transform the believer into the image of God, which is found in His law.

This is where many believers lose interest in God's plan. A common theme in biblical theology today is that, "the Law of God is abolished," but is this true? The answer is an emphatic no. The Messiah clearly states so in Matt. 5:17-18, "Think not that I am come to destroy the law, or the prophets: I am not come to destroy, but to fulfil. For verily I say unto you, till heaven and earth pass, one jot or one tittle shall in no wise pass from the law, till all be fulfilled." The Messiah himself declared the law to still be in full force and effect. If there is earth under your feet and a sky above your head, God's law is still here (Matt. 5:18). Paul even supports this as well when he said, "Do we then make void the law through faith? God forbid: yea, we establish the law" (Rom. 3:31). Paul was not advocating the abolishment of the Mosaic Law, like many seem to espouse, but rather Paul was saying that faith establishes the law. The word for "establish" is ἵστημι (histēmi) and means "to cause or make to stand."[40] The New Testament faith makes God's law to stand firm. This was even foretold by Isaiah when he stated the Messiah would, "magnify the law, and make it honorable" (Is. 42:21). To add even more evidence to our requirement to follow God's law, Solomon concludes in Ecclesiastes that we should, "Fear God, and keep his commandments: for this is the whole duty of man" (Eccl. 12:13). This is our duty before God, to keep His commandments.

---

[40] Thayer, Joseph H., "establish - ἁγιασμός - hagiasmos." *Thayer's Greek-English Lexicon of the New Testament,* Hendrickson Publishers Marketing 2014, pg. 307-308, G2476.

The question that logically follows is, how much of the law is man to follow? Is man required to practice all of God's law, or just part of God's law? Many people today would say that only the moral law is to be kept, but not the ceremonial law. The truth is, when the law is studied out it becomes clear that there is no ceremonial law at all. Every commandment and statute of God has a practical purpose for the individual and nation. Regarding how much of God's law is to be kept, however, the Messiah answered this question very clearly. In Matt. 5:19 the Messiah states, "Whosoever therefore shall break one of these least commandments, and shall teach men so, he shall be called the least in the kingdom of heaven: but whosoever shall do and teach them, the same shall be called great in the kingdom of heaven." The Messiah advocated practicing all of God's commandments, even the "least commandments." It is interesting to note that this is not justification, for he clearly stated that those who do not practice the least commandments will be "least in the kingdom of heaven." This does not mean they will not be part of the kingdom of heaven, but that they will have a lesser inheritance in the kingdom of heaven. Justification is free and cannot be earned. All those who practice faith in the Messiah will have a place in the kingdom of heaven, but our rewards in the kingdom are based upon our obedience to God's law. Remember, Solomon made this clear in Ecclesiastes when he finished with, "Fear God, and keep his commandments: for this is the whole duty of man. For God shall bring every work into judgment, with every secret thing, whether it be good, or whether it be evil" (Eccl. 12:13-14). God will judge our works of the law and that judgment will determine our rewards in the kingdom of heaven.

Other New Testament writers state the same principle. James mentioned a faith that was dead, because it was without works. In James 2:17-18 he states,

> Even so faith, if it has not works, is dead, being alone. Yes, a man may say, You have faith, and I have works: show me your faith without your works, and I will show you my faith by my works.

The context is clearly the works of the law. James 1:22-25 calls the Torah the "perfect law of liberty." James 2:1-9 speaks of showing respect of persons, which is a law from Lev. 19:5. James 2:8-11 speaks of fulfilling the "royal law" of love by keeping all the commandments. The entire book of James deals with God's law and our faith should lead us to practice that law. The works of the law is the evidence of our faith. Those who believe in the Messiah will seek out His will and follow it. The Messiah did not come to bring a new law, or even his own law, but to promote his Father's law. He only spoke what the Father gave him to speak (John 12:49-50).

James also mentions that the law acts the same as a mirror (James 1:22-25). One looks into a mirror to check their face to see if it is clean or dirty. If they find something wrong, they fix it. The Law of God is the same. Man is to look into the "perfect law of liberty" to see if they have anything to fix. This is sanctification. Man is to "study to show [them]selves approved unto God, a workman that needs not to be ashamed, rightly dividing the word of truth" as a means to live the life God called him to (2 Tim. 2:15). Man is not to use God's law to point the finger at others, but to use God's law to fix themselves. This is not justification, but sanctification.

Probably the clearest verses to define sanctification as learning to practice God's law is one that is usually quoted to demonstrate the opposite. The Apostle Paul said, "For by grace are you saved through faith; and that not of yourselves: it is the gift of God: Not of works, lest any man should boast" (Eph. 2:8-9). This is our justification and can only be attained by grace and faith, but the next verse clearly defines sanctification as the learning and practice of the Mosaic Law. Paul continues, "For we are his workmanship, created in Christ Jesus unto good works, which God has before ordained that we should walk in them" (Eph. 2:10). We are justified by grace alone, but after our justification we are created unto good works, "which God has before ordained that we should walk in them." The question to ask is this, when did God "before ordain" our good works to "walk" in? The answer is clearly found in the Mosaic Law. God mentions over and over again that His people should "walk" in His Law (Ex. 16:4, Ex. 18:20, Lev. 18:4, Lev. 26:3, Deut. 5:33, Deut. 8:6, Deut. 10:12-13, Deut. 11:22, Deut. 13:4-5, Deut. 19:9, Deut. 26:17, Deut. 28:9, Deut. 30:16, and many more). The Scripture makes this point very clear. In fact, the previous references are only from the Torah, but they are found dozens of times throughout the rest of the Old Testament as well. The only possible "good works" Paul could be speaking of is from the Law of God. Of course, this is right after justification by faith and grace.

In fact, the Greek word for sanctification is ἁγιάζω (hagiazō) or ἁγιασμός (hagiasmos), which means "to make holy" or to "purify."[41] This word is found throughout the Old Testament Greek Translation (Septuagint), which is the translation most often quoted by the Messiah and the New Testament writers. This word is most often used in the Old Testament to describe how God's people are sanctified when practicing His Law. In 1 Peter 1:15-16, the apostle is calling believers to "be ye holy; for I am holy." This is a direct quote from Lev. 11:44, which is the dietary chapter of the Torah. It is also found in Lev. 19:2, which is a chapter listing several statutes and commandments of the Torah. It is also found in Lev. 20:7-8. This verse straight out says that we are sanctified by God's law. "Sanctify yourselves therefore, and be ye holy: for I am YHVH your God. And you shall keep my statutes, and do them: I am YHVH which sanctify you." Either the apostle was misquoting the Scripture, which is highly doubtful, or New Testament believers are still required to keep God's commandments.

It is very unfortunate that most people who reject following God's law have usually never even studied God's law. Their view of the Law of God is usually that of the man-made fence laws of the Jews, which the Messiah rebuked for their improper understanding (Matt. 15:3-9). Perhaps if people would actually take a look at God's law they would not see it as a religious system, but a legal system. Someone should never pass judgment on the Mosaic Law until they have considered the entire matter (Prov. 18:13). The New and Old Testaments confirm that

---

[41] Strong, James, "Sanctification – ἁγιασμός - hagiasmos." *A Concise Dictionary of the Words in the Greek Bible*, pg. 7, G37 and 38.

the Torah is still to be practiced by the people of God. It is not for justification, but rather for sanctification.

This process called sanctification will take a lifetime, for Paul himself stated that, "he which has begun a good work in you will perform it until the day of Jesus Christ" (Phil. 1:6). We are to, "be transformed by the renewing of your mind, that you may prove what is that good, and acceptable, and perfect, will of God" (Rom. 12:2). The believer's responsibility in this lifetime is to, "work out our own salvation with fear and trembling. For it is God which works in [us] both to will and to do of his good pleasure" (Phil. 2:13-14). Sanctification is man working together with God to become the person He describes in His law. This will take a lifetime of study and devotion to God's word (2 Tim. 2:15). The ultimate end will be our glorification where God will remove this old decaying body of sin and replace it with a new spiritual body without sin (1 Cor. 15:42-44).

What is Glorification?

The third part of salvation is called glorification. The Greek word for glorification is δοξάζω (doxazō), which means "to honor" or "to magnify" or "to exalt to dignity."[42] It is translated fifty-one times as "glory/glorious/glorified", two times as "honor", and one time as "magnify." Where justification is a onetime act of God pardoning a sinner, and sanctification is a lifetime of working with God to become the person He wants man to be, glorification is the

---

[42] Strong, James, "glorification – δοξάζω - doxazō." *A Concise Dictionary of the Words in the Greek Bible*, pg. 24, G1392.

final product, the reward promised. It is the person a believer becomes in eternity.

When the Messiah returns, he will give believers a new body. This old body will be gone and a new one will be provided. In 1 Cor. 15:42-44 the Apostle Paul stated, "So also is the resurrection of the dead. It is sown in corruption; it is raised in incorruption: It is sown in dishonor; it is raised in glory: it is sown in weakness; it is raised in power: It is sown a natural body; it is raised a spiritual body. There is a natural body, and there is a spiritual body." The Messiah is the first fruits of creation. He is the first to be resurrected from the dead (1 Cor. 15:20-22). All those who practice faith in the Messiah (justification), will be molded into the person God desires (sanctification), and will ultimately be raised by him and given a new body when he returns (glorification).

The idea of a resurrection is not new. The ancient Hebrews believed in a resurrection and wrote about it. Job mentioned it in Job 19:25-26, "For I know that my redeemer lives, and that he shall stand at the latter day upon the earth: And though after my skin worms destroy this body, yet in my flesh shall I see God." Daniel mentioned in Dan. 12:2, "And many of them that sleep in the dust of the earth shall awake, some to everlasting life, and some to shame and everlasting contempt." In Psalm 49:15, the psalmist states, "But God will redeem my soul from the power of the grave: for he shall receive me." This concept is throughout the Old Testament and was alive and well during the Messiah's life. The Pharisees were constantly at odds with the Sadducees over the doctrine of a resurrection. The Sadducees did not believe in a resurrection and the Messiah corrected them saying, "But as touching the resurrection of the dead, have you not read that which was spoken unto you by God, saying, I am the God of Abraham, and the God of Isaac, and the God of Jacob? God is not the God of the dead, but of the living" (Matt. 22:31-32). This idea is further supported by the Apostle Paul in his first epistle to the Corinthians in chapter fifteen.

The fact that believers will be resurrected and given a new body is clear, the question then might be asked, what will this new body be like? Although these new bodies are referred to as spiritual bodies, this does not mean they are not physical. One way to tell is to look at what the Scripture says about the Messiah's resurrected body. First, it can be noted that he had a physical body. When Thomas doubted the Messiah, he was told to touch the Messiah's hands and side (John 20:27). Though this body is physical, it was also spiritual and could still apparently move through physical objects such as closed doors (John 20:19). This resurrection body is quite special. Along with being physical it is also "incorruptible," "glorious," and "powerful" (1 Cor. 15:42-44). This is God's ultimate goal, to rebuild what man's sin has destroyed. Along with a new body, God is also going to provide a new heaven and new earth (Is. 65:17). What amazing things God has in store for those who 'keep the commandments of God, and the faith of Jesus" (Rev. 14:12). As the Apostle Paul said, "Eye has not seen, nor ear heard, neither have entered into the heart of man, the things which God has prepared for them that love him" (1 Cor. 2:9).

What a great salvation God has given through the Messiah of Israel. God has done it all through the death, burial, and resurrection of the Messiah for justification. He works with man for sanctification to mold man into the person He wants them to be. And the final end for those who practice faith in the Messiah will be their glorification with a new body and the creation of a new heaven and a new earth. Oh, that man strives to not "neglect so great [a] salvation" (Heb. 2:3). The process of sanctification proves the necessity of God's law in our everyday lives, so why do so many reject it? Is there a benefit to keeping God's commandments? Did the church always reject the keeping of God's commandments or was there a time when the church followed the Law of God?

Chapter Four

Why Practice God's Law?

The question as to whether or not God's law should be practiced today is rarely asked. The mainstream Christian church almost unanimously rejects the Law of God. This has not always been the case, though. The Scripture teaches that the Law of God is good for man. Moses said it is "for our good always, that he might preserve us alive, as it is at this day." (Deut. 6:24). Every commandment in the Scripture is good for man, but for some reason this is not believed anymore. Most churches accept the Ten Commandments but reject the rest of God's commands. Some churches might accept a few more commandments, but eventually there is a line drawn where the church no longer keeps God's commandments. The truth is that God's law is endorsed in its entirety. Every commandment is for good and should be kept today. Perhaps the church's hesitation with this concept is the lack of understanding of all of God's commandments. This writer would contend that a proper understanding of God's commandments will demonstrate that all of God's law is relevant for today. Here are some verses that demonstrate what the Old Testament says.

What the Old Testament Says:

Here are just a few quotes to demonstrate that the Scriptures support of the Law of God.

> And YHVH **commanded us to do all these statutes**, to fear YHVH our God, **for our good always**, that he might **preserve us alive**, as it is at this day. (Deut. 6:4).

> If you walk in my **statutes**, and keep my **commandments**, and do them; **Then I will give you rain in due season**, and the land shall **yield her increase**, and the trees of the field shall **yield their fruit**. And your threshing shall reach unto the vintage, and the vintage shall reach unto the sowing time: and you shall eat your bread to the full, and dwell in your land safely. And I will give **peace in the land**, and you shall lie down, and none shall make you afraid: and I will rid evil beasts out of the land, neither shall the sword go through your land. And you shall chase your enemies, and they shall fall before you by the sword. And five of you shall chase a hundred, and a hundred of you shall put ten thousand to flight: and your enemies shall fall before you by the sword. **For I will have respect unto you**, and make you fruitful, and multiply you, and establish my covenant with you. And you shall eat old store, and bring forth the old because of the new. And I will set my

tabernacle among you: and my soul shall not abhor you. And I will walk among you, and will be your God, and you shall be my people (Lev. 26:5-12).

And it shall come to pass, if you shall hearken diligently unto the voice of YHVH your God, to **observe and to do all his commandments** which I command you this day, that YHVH your **God will set you on high above all nations of the earth**: And **all these blessings shall come on you**, and overtake you, if you shall hearken unto the voice of YHVH your God (Deut. 28:1-2).

With my whole heart have I sought you: **O let me not wander from your commandments**. Your word have I hid in my heart, that I might not sin against you. Blessed art you, O YHVH: **teach me your statutes** (Psalms 119:10-12).

I will run the way of your commandments, when you shall enlarge my heart. **Teach me, O YHVH, the way of your statutes; and I shall keep it unto the end**. Give me understanding, and **I shall keep your law**; yes, I shall observe it with my whole heart. Make me to go in the path of your commandments; for therein do I delight (Psalms 119:34-35).

Clearly the Old Testament endorses the practice of God's law. There are many more verses that would state the same as those above, but since very few people object to the statement that the Old Testament endorses the Law of God, there is no need to quote any more. However, for those that would say that these quotes are only from the Old Testament, but now is the time of the New Testament, here are some New Testament quotes to consider. Keep in mind, however, that the church in the New Testament did not have a New Testament Bible yet. They only had the Old Testament, which is what they called the Scripture. They believed and followed the Old Testament Scriptures because they did not have the New Testament Scriptures yet. Please consider the following quotes from the New Testament. Here is what the Messiah, the apostles, and the early church fathers said about the Law of God.

What the Messiah Said:

- The Messiah clearly taught and advocated practicing God's law. In Matthew 5:17, he stated that he did not, "come to destroy the law, or the prophets: **I am not come to destroy, but to fulfil.**"

- The Messiah was so emphatic about the above statement that he said "Till heaven and earth pass, **one jot or one tittle shall in no wise pass from the law,** till all be fulfilled." (Matthew 5:18) If there is an earth beneath, and a sky above, God's law is still in effect. He even advocated every "jot" and "tittle" of the law. This is equivalent to saying every dot of an "i" or crossing of a "t".

Jesus/Yeshua teaching a crowd.

- As if this was not enough, the Messiah added that even the "least commandments" were still in effect. In Matthew 5:20, he states "Whosoever therefore shall **break one of these least commandments**, and shall teach men so, he shall be called the least in the kingdom of heaven: but whosoever shall do and teach them, the same shall be called great in the kingdom of heaven."

- And he said unto him, why call you me good? there is none good but one, that is, God: but if you will enter into life, **keep the commandments** (Matt. 19:17).

- If you love me, **keep my commandments** (John 14:15).

- **He that has my commandments, and keeps them**, he it is that loves me: and he that loves me shall be loved of my Father, and I will love him, and will manifest myself to him (John 14:21).

- **If you keep my commandments, you shall abide in my love**; even as I have kept my Father's commandments, and abide in his love (John 15:10).

- In fact, the Old Testament clearly taught that the Messiah "will **magnify the law**, and make it honorable." (Is. 42:21) This is exactly what he did. He came to explain the spirit of the law, or rather, the proper understanding of the law.

It is quite clear that the Messiah supported following God's law. Nonetheless, many people still place the Gospels under the Old Covenant and consider these statements to be for those under the Old Covenant, but not those under the New Covenant. This simply is not true.

The question then is, did the apostles endorse following God's law? Without any doubt they did. Consider the following:

What the Apostles Said:

The Apostle Paul endorsed God's law:
- Paul starts his epistle to the Romans by stating, "For not the hearers of the law are just before God, but **the doers of the law** shall be justified" (Rom. 2:13).

- After Paul finished a summary on faith and salvation through grace, he said "Do we then make void the law through faith? **God forbid**: yes, **we establish the law**" (Rom. 3:31).

- Paul later speaks of the laws' place regarding sin and concludes that "the **law is holy**, and the **commandment holy**, and just, and good" (Rom. 7:12).

The Apostles

The Apostle John endorsed God's law:

- And hereby we do know that we know him, **if we keep his commandments**. He that says, I know him, and keeps not his commandments, is a liar, and the truth is not in him. (1 John 2:3-4).

- John concludes this statement by saying, "He that says he abides in him ought himself also so **to walk, even as he walked**" (1 John 3:6). Didn't the Messiah "fulfill" all the law and walk accordingly?   God's people should do the same.

- John also gives us the biblical definition of sin; "Whosoever commits sin transgresses also the law: for **sin is the transgression of the law**" (1 John 3:4). If transgressing God's law is sin, should believers continue in sin (break God's law) after they have been forgiven? God forbid. (Rom. 6:1-2).

- John states later that "whatsoever we ask, we receive of him, because we **keep his commandments**, and do those things that are pleasing in his sight" (1 John 3:22). What is pleasing in God's sight? The keeping of His commandments.

- He concludes his epistle by telling us what love is, "By this we know that we love the children of God, when we love God, and keep his commandments. For this is the love of God, that we **keep his commandments**: and his commandments are not grievous" (1 John 5:2-3).

- Here is the patience of the saints: **here are they that keep the commandments of God**, and the faith of Jesus (Rev. 14:12).

- **Blessed are they that do his commandments**, that they may have right to the tree of life, and may enter in through the gates into the city (Rev. 22:14).

The Apostle Peter endorsed God's law:

- The High Priest asked the apostles concerning their "doctrine" (law) and Peter's response was "We ought to **obey God** rather than men." (Acts 5:29)

- Peter mentioned, "Instead, **be holy in every aspect of your life**, just as the one who called you is holy. For it is written, "You must be holy, because I am holy." (1 Peter 1:15-16). This is a quote from a few different places in God's law.

  - Lev. 11:44 - 46: "For I am YHVH your God: you shall therefore sanctify yourselves, and **you shall be holy; for I am holy**. For I am YHVH that brings you up out of the land of Egypt, to be your God: you shall therefore be holy, for I am holy. This is the law of the beasts, and of the fowl, and of every living creature that moves in the waters, and of every creature that creeps upon the earth."

  - Lev. 19:2: "Speak unto all the congregation of the children of Israel, and say unto them, **You shall be holy: for I YHVH your God am holy**."

- o Lev. 20:26: "**And you shall be holy unto me: for I YHVH am holy**, and have severed you from other people, that you should be mine."

- o Lev. 21:8: "You shall sanctify him therefore; for he offers the bread of your God: **he shall be holy unto you: for I YHVH, which sanctify you, am holy**."

  - ▪ Either Peter was misquoting Leviticus or he was taking it completely out of context. Each of these verses reference the need to practice God's law to be holy, because YHVH is holy. If Peter is quoting Leviticus correctly and not out of context, then he is saying the "behavior" needed to be holy is to follow God's laws.

- In 1 Peter 2:9 Peter says, "But you are a chosen generation, a royal priesthood, a holy nation, a peculiar people; that you should show forth the praises of him who has called you out of darkness into his marvelous light." What most people don't realize that this is a quote from God's law. Just look at the following verses:

  - o We are chosen: "YHVH your **God has chosen you** to be a special people unto himself, above all people that are upon the face of the earth" (Deut. 7:6).

- o We are a priesthood: "And you shall be unto me a **kingdom of priests**, and a holy nation" (Ex. 19:6).

- o We are a holy nation: "And you shall be unto me a kingdom of priests, and a **holy nation**" (Ex. 19:6).

- o We are a peculiar people: "then you shall be a **peculiar treasure** unto me above all people" (Ex. 19:5) . . . "and YHVH has chosen you to be a **peculiar people** unto himself" (Deut. 14:2) . . . "And YHVH has avouched you this day to be his **peculiar people**" (Deut. 26:18).

  - ▪ Was Peter misquoting the Scripture, or are New Testament believers a "chosen" people, a royal "priesthood", a "holy nation", and a "peculiar people" because they practice God's law? One thing is certain, those who practice God's law instead of man's law, will be "peculiar." Those who practice the Feast of Tabernacles instead of Christmas sure are peculiar. Those who practice the Passover instead of Easter sure are peculiar. The more you practice of God's law, the more peculiar you will become.

It is clear that the New Testament writers endorsed following God's law. Each of them stated so clearly. From the smallest books like First and Second John to the larger books like Romans and Hebrews the evidence is clear. It is also very clear that the Messiah himself endorsed the Law of God. The Messiah and the apostles quoted the Old Testament over four hundred times and they directly stated the need to follow it. They quoted the law directly over two hundred times. For even more evidence, take a look at what the early church fathers taught about the Law of God.

What the Early Church Fathers Said:

Ignatius of Antioch: First Century CE

*For they speak of Christ, not that they may preach Christ, but that they may reject Christ; and they speak of the law, **not that they may establish the law**, but that they may proclaim things contrary to it. For they alienate Christ from the Father, **and the law from Christ**.*[43]

*It is fitting, therefore, that ye should keep aloof from such persons, and neither in private nor in public to talk with them; **but to give heed to the law**, and the prophets, and to those who have preached to you the word of salvation.*[44]

---

[43] *Ante-Nicene Fathers*, Volume 1, Ignatius, Epistle to the Trallians, Chapter 11, 29-30.

[44] *Ante-Nicene Fathers*, Volume 1, Ignatius, Epistle to the Smyrnaeans, Chapter 7, 20-21.)

Polycarp of Smyrna: 69 – 155 CE

*Knowing, then, that "God is not mocked," **we ought to walk worthy of His commandment and glory**. In like manner should the deacons be blameless before the face of His righteousness, as being the servants of God and Christ, and not of men. They **must not be slanderers, double-tongued, or lovers of money**, but temperate in all things, compassionate, industrious, walking according to the truth of the Lord, who was the servant of all.*[45]

Clement of Rome: 35-99 CE

*Those, therefore, who present their offerings at the appointed times, are accepted and blessed; **for inasmuch as they follow the laws of the Lord, they sin not**. For his own peculiar services are assigned to the high priest, and their own proper place is prescribed to the priests, and their own special ministrations devolve on the Levites. **The layman is bound by the laws that pertain to laymen**. Let every one of you, brethren, give thanks to God in his own order, living in all good conscience, with becoming gravity, and not going beyond the rule of the ministry prescribed to him.*[46]

*Let us then, men and brethren, with all energy act the part of soldiers, **in accordance with His holy commandments**.*[47]

---

[45] *Ante-Nicene Fathers*, Volume 1, Polycarp, Epistle to the Philippians, chapter 5

[46] *Ante-Nicene Fathers*, Volume 1, Clement of Rome, Epistle to the Corinthians, Chapter 40

[47] *Ante-Nicene Fathers*, Volume 1, Clement of Rome, Epistle to the Corinthians, Chapter 37

*Blessed are we, beloved, **if we keep the commandments of God** in the harmony of love; that so through love our sins may be forgiven us.*[48]

Theophilus of Antioch: Second Century CE

*For **God has given us a law and holy commandments**; and everyone who keeps these can be saved, and, obtaining the resurrection, can inherit incorruption.*[49]

Clemente of Alexandria: Second Century CE

*Wherefore let us **regard the Word as law**, and **His commands and counsels as the short and straight paths to immortality**; for His precepts are full of persuasion, not of fear.*[50]

*Whence **the law was rightly said to have been given by Moses**, being a **rule of right and wrong**; and we may call it with accuracy the divine ordinance, inasmuch as it was given by God through Moses.*[51]

***For the law**, in its solicitude for those who obey, trains up to piety, and prescribes what is to be done, and **restrains each one from sins**, imposing penalties even on lesser sins. . . . But it is the highest and most perfect good, when one is able to lead back any one from the practice of evil to virtue and well-doing, **which is the very function of the law**. . . . **To know the law is characteristic of a good disposition**. And again: "Wicked men do not understand the law; but they who*

---

[48] *Ante-Nicene Fathers*, Volume 1, Clement of Rome, Epistle to the Corinthians, Chapter 37

[49] *Ante-Nicene Fathers*, Volume 2, Theophilus, To Autolycus, Book 2, Chapter 27

[50] *Ante-Nicene Fathers*, Volume 2, Clement, Instructor, Book 1, Chapter 3

[51] *Ante-Nicene Fathers*, Volume 2, Clement of Alexandria – Stramata, Book 1, Chapter 26

> *seek the Lord shall have understanding in all that is good.*[52]

These early church fathers, as well as many others, endorsed the Law of God for the church of their day. After all, the only Scriptures they had was what is called the Old Testament today. The Law of God is a big part of those Scriptures. It is contained in the first five books of the Bible called the Torah. However, the law is also spread throughout the rest of the Scripture as well. In fact, this writer believes that the whole Bible is a law book, from Genesis to Revelation. The point here is that God's law is a major part of the Scriptures, but it is also one of the least studied topics. If the church today would study God's law they would understand the enormous benefits ascribed to it. For example, most do not realize that the Scripture says nothing negative regarding God's law. Those passages used to discredit the law are taken off point and out of context. The truth is the Scriptures endorse God's law from beginning to end. It is important to remember that God's law is good for man and brings many blessings to those who are obedient. This can be seen throughout the Scripture from Genesis to Revelation, but for some reason the church today does not accept this. Here is a quick survey of the many blessings for keeping the commandments of YHVH and some of the curses for not keeping the commandments of YHVH.

---

[52] *Ante-Nicene Fathers*, Volume 2, Clement of Alexandria – Stramata, Book 1, Chapter 27

The Benefits of Practicing God's Law:

Both the Old and New Testament endorse the keeping of God's commandments, but this does not provide the entire answer to the question of this chapter. Why practice God's Law? It answers the question, "Does the Bible endorse the practice of God's law?" Yes, it does. However, the question of why a believer, church, or nation should practice God's law has not yet been fully answered. This question of why is answered when studying the blessings and curses of God's law. These blessings and curses are found primarily in Leviticus 26 and Deuteronomy 28. It is here where the true answer to this question is derived. Here is a quick summary of the blessings and curses of God's law.

These chapters start out with God presenting Israel with a choice. That choice is obedience or disobedience to His commandments. Here is one such choice.

> **If you walk in my statutes, and keep my commandments**, and do them; **Then I will give you** rain in due season, **and** the land shall yield her increase, **and** the trees of the field shall yield their fruit. **And** your threshing shall reach unto the vintage, **and** the vintage shall reach unto the sowing time: **and** you shall eat your bread to the full, **and** dwell in your land safely. **And** I will give peace in the land, **and** you shall lie down, **and** none shall make you afraid: **and** I will rid evil beasts out of the land, neither shall the sword go through your land. **And** you shall chase your enemies, **and** they shall fall before you by the sword. **And** five of you shall chase a hundred, **and** a hundred of you shall put ten thousand to flight: **and** your enemies shall fall before you by the

> sword. For I will have respect unto you, **and** make you fruitful, and multiply you, **and** establish my covenant with you. **And** you shall eat old store, **and** bring forth the old because of the new. **And** I will set my tabernacle among you: **and** my soul shall not abhor you. **And** I will walk among you, **and** will be your God, **and** you shall be my people. I am YHVH your God, which brought you forth out of the land of Egypt, that you should not be their bondmen; **and** I have broken the bands of your yoke, **and** made you go upright. (Lev. 26:3-13)

This is the first part of the choice God gave to Israel and is referred to as the blessings of the covenant. If Israel chooses to obey God and keep His commandments and statutes, then God will bring many blessings upon Israel. These blessings focus on the success of that nation. Keeping YHVH's commandments will lead to a blessed nation. The next section gives the curses, or penalties, of breaking God's commandments.

> But **if you will not hearken unto me, and will not do all these commandments**; And **if you shall despise my statutes**, or **if your soul abhor my judgments**, so that you will not do all my commandments, but that **you break my covenant**: I also will do this unto you; **I will** even appoint over you terror, consumption, and the burning ague, that shall consume the eyes, and cause sorrow of heart: and **you shall** sow your seed in vain, for your enemies shall eat it. And **I will** set my face against you, and **you shall** be slain before your enemies: they that hate you shall reign over you; and **you shall** flee when none pursue you. And if you will not yet for all this hearken unto me, then **I will** punish you seven times more for your sins. And **I will** break the pride of your power; and **I will** make

> your heaven as iron, and your earth as brass: And
> your strength shall be spent in vain: for your land
> shall not yield her increase, neither shall the trees
> of the land yield their fruits. (Lev. 26:14-20)

This is referred to as the curse of the law, which today would be called the penalty of the law. In fact, the rest of the chapter contains several more verses with many more curses. These curses, or penalties, refer to the discipline God will give Israel when they disobey. It is these blessings and curses that is the real reason a nation should keep the commandments of YHVH. Obedience to God's law will build a strong nation. Disobedience to God's law will only weaken a nation. This is simply a natural process because the blessings mentioned are the natural affect of keeping God's commandments, and the curses mentioned are the natural affect of not keeping God's commandments. In fact, this writer has often said, "The rise and fall of every nation is the transition from obedience to disobedience of the Law of God."

In summary, the New Testament writers and the Messiah himself endorsed the Law of God. They quoted it over four hundred times and they directly stated the need to follow it. Even our early church fathers supported the Law of God. The reason God's law is so endorsed in the Bible and church history are the many blessings for keeping it. The question then is, why do so many people believe that God's law has been abolished? Is this unwarranted, or is there a reason to think so? This writer readily admits that there are some verses that might sound like God has removed His law, but is this true? Perhaps there is another way to look at these verses so as not to have the Bible seemingly contradict itself. The next chapter will cover some common verses used to say that God's law is abolished and will demonstrate a different understanding of those verses. The purpose of this book series is to place the Law of God in the right scriptural context and provide a practical understanding of that law and how it fits in the New Testament and today. When God's law is understood correctly the church should rightly accept and keep all of God's commandments.

Chapter Five

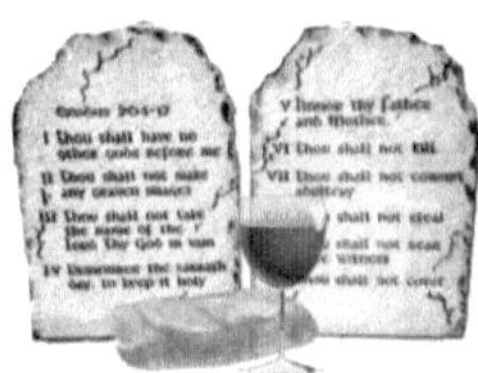

Difficult New Testament Passages

Although it is very clear that the New Testament, as well as the Old Testament, fully support the keeping of God's law, there are some difficult passages that need to be addressed. These passages are commonly used within the church to undermine the need to keep the commandments of God. Most of these verses are from the Apostle Paul. Many of his writings appear to say that God's law is abolished, but Paul's writings can often be hard to understand.   In fact, the Apostle Peter warned us regarding the writings of Paul. Peter said,

> And think of the long-suffering of our Lord as salvation, as our beloved brother Paul also has written to you according to the wisdom given to him as also in all his letters, speaking in them of these things; **in which are some things hard to be understood, which the unlearned and unstable**

pervert, as also they do the rest of the Scriptures, to their own destruction. (2 Pet. 3:15-16)

Remember, Peter is not refuting the writings of Paul, but warning us to make sure we have a correct understanding. Peter says that Paul's writings are "hard to be understood." Peter also says that the "unlearned and unstable pervert" Paul's writings, which implies that Paul was apparently learned and stable. It might be asked, what was Paul learned and stable in? Here is a quick resume of the Apostle Paul; he was "Circumcised the eighth day, of the stock of Israel, of the tribe of Benjamin, a Hebrew of the Hebrews; as touching the law, a Pharisee; concerning zeal, persecuting the church; touching the righteousness which is in the law, blameless" (Phil. 3:5-6), and educated at the "feet of Gamaliel" (Acts 22:3). The Apostle Paul was well educated in the Mosaic Law. He would be what we would call today a prosecuting attorney for he was sent out by the High Priest to persecute, or prosecute, the church (Acts 9:1-2). In modern times, this would be like talking to a lawyer about a specific legal matter. Their understanding is going to be head and shoulders above a layperson's understanding. In the Apostle Paul's day, the layperson would have a hard time understanding his writings because they are, "unlearned and unstable" in the Mosaic Law. Even the Apostle Peter had a hard time understanding Paul's writings. Those who say Paul advocated the abolishment of the Mosaic Law are "unlearned and unstable" in that law. It is important to use the Mosaic Law to properly understand Paul's writings. In so doing, it will be clear that he never once advocated the abolishment of God's law, but rather endorsed the proper understanding and practice of it. The truth is, with proper study, each of the passages in the New Testament that seems to say God's law is abolished really does not say this. In many cases they actually state the contrary. Here are a few such passages that are commonly used to say that the Law of God is abolished. Although most of these verses are writings from the Apostle Paul, a good place to start is the Jerusalem Council found in the book of Acts, which was written by the physician, Luke.

The Jerusalem Council (Acts 15):

The question of whether or not to keep God's commandments is not new. The fact of the matter is that the apostles dealt with this question early in the life of the church. A meeting was held and a decision was made. The end result of this meeting was the upholding of God's law. Ironically, it is this very meeting that many today use to endorse the idea that the Law of God has been abolished. This couldn't be further from the truth. In fact, this meeting specifically upheld God's law in light of grace. Here is the passage in its entirety with the controversial portion in bold.

> And certain men which came down from Judaea taught the brethren, and said, **Except you be circumcised after the manner of Moses, you cannot be saved**. When therefore Paul and Barnabas had no small dissension and disputation with them, they determined that Paul and Barnabas, and certain other of them, should go up to Jerusalem unto the apostles and elders about this question. And being brought on their way by the church, they passed through Phenice and

Samaria, declaring the conversion of the Gentiles: and they caused great joy unto all the brethren. And when they were come to Jerusalem, they were received of the church, and of the apostles and elders, and they declared all things that God had done with them. But there rose up certain of the sect of the Pharisees which believed, saying, that it was needful to circumcise them, and to command them to keep the law of Moses. And the apostles and elders came together for to consider of this matter. And when there had been much disputing, Peter rose up, and said unto them, Men and brethren, you know how that a good while ago God made choice among us, that the Gentiles by my mouth should hear the word of the gospel, and believe. And God, which knows the hearts, bare them witness, giving them the Holy Spirit, even as he did unto us; And put no difference between us and them, purifying their hearts by faith. Now therefore why tempt ye God, to put a yoke upon the neck of the disciples, which neither our fathers nor we were able to bear? But we believe that through the grace of the Lord Jesus Christ we shall be saved, even as they. Then all the multitude kept silence, and gave audience to Barnabas and Paul, declaring what miracles and wonders God had wrought among the Gentiles by them. And after they had held their peace, James answered, saying, Men and brethren, hearken unto me: Simeon has declared how God at the first did visit the Gentiles, to take out of them a people for his name. And to this agree the words of the prophets; as it is written, After this I will return, and will build again the tabernacle of David, which is fallen down; and I will build again the ruins thereof, and I will set it up: That the residue of men might seek after the Lord, and all the

Gentiles, upon whom my name is called, says the Lord, who does all these things. Known unto God are all his works from the beginning of the world. **Wherefore my sentence is, that we trouble not them, which from among the Gentiles are turned to God: But that we write unto them, that they abstain from pollutions of idols, and from fornication, and from things strangled, and from blood**. For Moses of old time has in every city them that preach him, being read in the synagogues every sabbath day. (Acts 15:1-21)

At first glance this might appear to dismiss the need to keep the commandments of God. However, a thorough review will show the opposite is true. In Acts 15, we read of a group of Jews who are troubling Gentile believers to be circumcised and practice the Mosaic Law. These Jews are telling the Gentiles, "Except you be circumcised after the manner of Moses, you cannot be saved" (Acts 15:1). This was troubling the Gentile believers. Since Paul and Barnabas "had no small dissension and disputation" with the Gentiles, it was determined that they should go to Jerusalem to determine this matter (Acts 15:2). As Paul and Barnabas traveled to Jerusalem their message of the Gentile conversion was received with great joy in all the cities they visited, including Jerusalem (Acts 15:3-4). When they finally reached Jerusalem, they encountered the problem before them. "There rose up certain of the sect of the Pharisees which believed, saying, that it was needful to circumcise them, and to command them to keep the law of Moses" (Acts 15:5). The Pharisees, who caused the Messiah great trouble (Matt. 15:3-9), were doing the same to the Gentile believers. Though these

Pharisees were believers, they still held some of their old doctrines that caused division (Matt. 16:6). This caused the apostles and elders to discuss the matter before them (Acts 15:6).

The Apostle Peter rose up to speak first on this matter. "Men and brethren, you know how that a good while ago God made choice among us, that the Gentiles by my mouth should hear the word of the gospel, and believe. And God, which knows the hearts, bare them witness, giving them the Holy Spirit, even as he did unto us; And put no difference between us and them, purifying their hearts by faith" (Acts 15:7-9). Peter points out the proof of their faith, that of the Holy Spirit. After all, one of the purposes of the Holy Spirit was to put the "seal" of proof on our salvation (2 Cor. 1:22, Eph. 1:13). No one can doubt that the Gentiles are accepted by faith, even though they are not circumcised. Peter concluded with, "Now therefore why tempt ye God, to put a yoke upon the neck of the disciples, which neither our fathers nor we were able to bear? But we believe that through the grace of the Lord Jesus Christ we shall be saved, even as they" (Acts 15:10-11). The Pharisees are putting a burden on the Gentiles that is impossible. In fact, they themselves could not carry that same burden. This burden was that of following God's law to earn salvation. This is contrary to grace and contrary to the gospel of the Messiah.

Keep in mind, this is not saying that practicing God's law is not good. Remember, salvation comes in three parts: Justification, sanctification, and glorification. It is not possible to be justified by the Law of God because every person has already failed (James 2:10), but this is what the Pharisees believed, which led to their downfall. Justification can only be received by faith in the death, burial, and resurrection of the Messiah. Sanctification is after justification. Once someone is justified and forgiven of their sins they now have a whole life ahead of them to become the person God wants them to be. This is where the Law of God comes in. God's law does not make someone righteous, but it does define righteousness. Sanctification is where man works together with God to learn His Law and apply it to their life. This will become clearer as we continue.

After Peter spoke, the crowd marveled at how the Holy Spirit worked through Paul and Barnabas. The crowd listened as Paul and Barnabas confirmed Peter's statement (Acts 15:12). Then James stood up to conclude the discussion and make a judgment on the matter. James confirms the words of Peter (Acts 15:14) and then points to the prophets to confirm Peter's words.

> And to this agree the words of the prophets; as it is written, After this I will return, and will build again the tabernacle of David, which is fallen down; and I will build again the ruins thereof, and I will set it up: That the residue of men might seek after the Lord, and all the Gentiles, upon whom my name is called, says the Lord, who does all these things (Acts 15:16-17).

James shows how God's word declared that the Gentiles would be part of salvation. In fact, the law confirms this as well. God has always allowed Gentiles to come into His people and practice His Law (Ex. 12:49, Ex. 22:2, Ex. 23:9). This is nothing new and probably what James meant in Acts 15:18 when he said, "Known unto God are all his works from the beginning of the world." James then makes his judgment on this matter.

"Wherefore my sentence is, that we trouble not them, which from among the Gentiles are turned to God: But that we write unto them, that they abstain from pollutions of idols, and from fornication, and from things strangled, and from blood" (Acts 15:19-20). At first glance, it sounds like James is making light of the Mosaic Law. We are not to bother the Gentiles with the Mosaic Law, especially concerning circumcision. However, he does mention some laws that the Gentiles should follow. Apparently, idolatry, adultery (fornication) and some of the dietary laws (strangled and blood) are among the laws that Gentiles should follow. This seems odd because James does not appear to give any reason for why the Gentiles should follow these laws and not others. An interesting question to ask is, why did James say the Gentiles should follow dietary laws, but today the church does not? It is interesting to note that the modern church uses this very passage to demonstrate that the Law of God is abolished. This is unfortunate for this passage says no such thing. In fact, it is clearly endorsing some laws that the church rejects today. When you read the very next verse you find out why James required some laws, but not apparently others.

The next verse states, "For Moses of old time has in every city them that preach him, being read in the synagogues every Sabbath day" (Acts 15:21). The word translated as "for" is the Greek word γάρ (gar/for), which means, "assigning a reason (used in argument)."[53] This means the reason for keeping only these four laws is in the next verse. James is not saying that the Law of God is abolished or that it should only be followed in part. James is saying to only hold the Gentiles to these laws (idolatry, adultery, and dietary) for now, after all, they have every Sabbath day to hear Moses preached in the Synagogue to learn the rest of God's law. James is pointing out a good starting point to practice God's law. Each of these commandments were commonly broken in the first century. These four are a great place to start, especially for the audience he was speaking to. A different set of commandments might be recommended for new believers today. James is emphasizing that God is not providing grace to break God's law, but rather grace to learn God's law. It is absurd to expect anyone to stop practicing their previous law and start practicing all of God's law the very next moment. There is grace to learn God's law and apply it to their lives. As the Gentiles started going to the Synagogue on the Sabbath day they were to start applying more and more of God's laws to their lives.

The Apostles agreed with James' judgment and sent letters to all the churches confirming this doctrine (Acts 15:22-29). This doctrine is simple. We do not have grace to break God's law, but rather we have grace to learn God's law and apply it to our lives. As we grow in the knowledge of God and His law, we are required to practice more and more of those laws. This chapter in the book of Acts is a great demonstration of how the Law of God and

---

[53] Strong, James, "for – γάρ - gar." *A Concise Dictionary of the Words in the Greek Bible*, pg. 20, G1063.

grace fit together. Remember, God looks at the heart of man (1 Sam. 16:7). He knows if someone's heart's desire is to follow Him or not. Those who want to follow after God will seek His Law and follow it to the best of their ability. When someone can't follow a certain law, there is grace as needed. As the Apostle Paul said, "For the grace of God that bringeth salvation hath appeared to all men, Teaching us that, denying ungodliness and worldly lusts, we should live soberly, righteously, and godly, in this present world" (Titus 2:11-12). There is not only grace for justification, but there is grace for sanctification as well. God has an abundance of grace to forgive man of his sins, but He also has an abundance of grace to help man become the person he is supposed to be.

The Law Was Our Schoolmaster (Gal. 3):

Galatians 3 is another passage of Scripture commonly used to demonstrate the removal of God's law for the church today. In fact, often the entire book is mentioned to support the notion that the Law of God is abolished. Regardless, a thorough study will demonstrate the exact opposite. It is very fitting to discuss the book of Galatians right after the Jerusalem Counsel of Acts 15. Paul is dealing with the same Pharisees from Acts 15 and there are very similar themes throughout each passage. A good understanding of the Jerusalem Council is helpful when trying to understand the book of Galatians, especially chapter three. Here is a quick look at Galatians 3 with the controversial verses in bold.

O foolish Galatians, who has bewitched you, that you should not obey the truth, before whose eyes Jesus Christ has been evidently set forth, crucified among you? This only would I learn of you, Received you the Spirit by the works of the law, or by the hearing of faith? Are you so foolish? having begun in the Spirit, are you now made perfect by the flesh? Have you suffered so many things in vain? if it be yet in vain. He therefore that ministers to you the Spirit, and works miracles among you, does he do it by the works of the law, or by the hearing of faith? Even as Abraham believed God, and it was accounted to him for righteousness. Know ye therefore that they which are of faith, the same are the children of Abraham. And the Scripture, foreseeing that God would justify the heathen through faith, preached before the gospel unto Abraham, saying, in you shall all nations be blessed. So then they which are of faith are blessed with faithful Abraham. For as many as are of the works of the law are under the curse: for it is written, cursed is every one that continues not in all things which are written in the book of the law to do them. But that no man is justified by the law in the sight of God, it is evident: for, the just shall live by faith. And the law is not of faith: but, the man that does them shall live in them. Christ has redeemed us from the curse of the law, being made a curse for us: for it is written, cursed is every one that hangs on a tree: That the blessing of Abraham might come on the Gentiles through Jesus Christ; that we might receive the promise of the Spirit through faith. Brethren, I speak after the manner of men; Though it be but a man's covenant, yet if it be confirmed, no man disannuls, or adds thereto. Now to Abraham and his seed were the promises made. He says not, and to seeds, as of many; but as of one, and to your seed, which is Christ. And this I say, that the covenant, that was confirmed before of God in Christ, the law, which was four hundred and thirty years after, cannot disannul, that it should make the promise of none effect. For if the inheritance be of the law, it is no more of promise: but God gave it to Abraham by promise. **Wherefore then serves the law? It was added because of transgressions, till the seed should come to whom the promise was made**; and it was ordained by angels in the hand of a mediator. Now a mediator is not a mediator of one, but God is one. Is the law then against the promises of God? God forbid: for if there had been a law given which could have given life, verily righteousness should have been by the law. But the Scripture has concluded all under sin, that the promise by faith of Jesus Christ might be given to them that believe. But before faith came, we were kept under the law, shut up unto the faith which should afterwards be revealed. **Wherefore the law was our schoolmaster to bring us unto Christ, that we might be justified by faith. But after that faith is come, we are no longer under a schoolmaster.** For you are all the children of God by faith in Christ Jesus. For as many of you as have been baptized into Christ have put on Christ. There is neither Jew nor Greek, there is neither bond nor free, there is neither male nor female: for you are all one in Christ Jesus and if ye be Christ's, then are you Abraham's seed, and heirs according to the promise. (Gal. 3:1-29)

The chapter starts out with a reminder, "O foolish Galatians, who has bewitched you, that you should not obey the truth, before whose eyes Jesus Christ has been evidently set forth, crucified among you? This only would I learn of you, Received you the Spirit by the works of the law, or by the hearing of faith" (Gal. 3:1-2). The Galatians, as all true believers, received the Holy Spirit by faith and not the works of the law. Paul continues, "Are you so foolish? having begun in the Spirit, are you now made perfect by the flesh" (Gal. 3:3-4). This verse is often used to show that following the law after faith is foolish, but it says no such thing. The Galatians were going back to the "circumcision" requirements of the Pharisees. Earlier in the book they were called "false brethren" (Gal. 2:4), who "seemed to be somewhat" (Gal. 2:6), they were "of the circumcision" (Gal. 2:7-9), they were from Judea (Acts 15:1), they were of the "sect of the Pharisees" (Acts 15:5), they claimed to be believers (Acts 15:5), they believed you must be circumcised prior to salvation (Acts 15:1), and they did so that they may "glory in their flesh" (Gal. 6:12-13). The Galatians were being influenced by these Pharisees and the end result is giving up faith for the practice of the law to earn salvation. Instead, they should have faith first and practice God's law through sanctification.

Paul continues, "He therefore that ministers to you the Spirit, and works miracles among you, does he do it by the works of the law, or by the hearing of faith" (Gal. 3:5). All of the miracles among the Galatians came by the Holy Spirit through their faith, not through their works. Paul then quotes Gen. 15:6 to use Abraham as an example of faith, "Even as Abraham believed God, and it was accounted to him for righteousness. Know therefore that they which are of faith, the same are the children of Abraham" (Gal. 3:6-7). The Galatians have become children of Abraham through their faith, not their works. This is their justification. Their faith has given them their righteousness. Though Abraham was the epitome of faith, he was also the epitome of works. In Genesis 26:4-5, God tells Isaac where the place of works is in salvation.

> And I will make your seed to multiply as the stars of heaven, and will give unto your seed all these countries; and in your seed shall all the nations of the earth be blessed; Because that Abraham **obeyed my voice**, and **kept my charge**, **my commandments**, **my statutes**, and **my laws**. (Gen. 26:4-5)

Abraham was justified (accounted to him for righteousness) by his faith (Gen. 15:6), but the blessings came because he "obeyed [God's] voice, and kept [God's] charge, [God's] commandments, [God's] statutes, and [God's] laws" (Gen. 26:4-5). This is the difference between justification and sanctification. Justification is by faith alone, but sanctification comes by works and the keeping of God's commandments. This is the maturing process of sanctification and it takes an entire lifetime.

The Messiah also adds to this understanding when answering the Pharisees in John 8:39, "If you were Abraham's children, you would do the works of Abraham." You see, faith comes first, then the works of the law. This is how Abraham kept God's laws. He started with faith first, then obedience came as the fruit of his faith. This is what James was speaking of in James 2:17-18 when he said, "Even so faith, if it has not works, is dead, being alone. Yes, a man may say, You have faith, and I have works: show me your faith without your works, and I will show you my faith by my works." The end result of true faith will be the desire to follow God's law (works of the law). James sums up his arguments by saying, "See how faith wrought with his works, and by works was faith made perfect? And the Scripture was fulfilled which says, Abraham believed God, and it was imputed unto him for righteousness: and he was called the Friend of God" (James 2:22-23). James put justification and sanctification in its rightful place. Abraham's works of the law was the evidence of his true faith. The Galatians started this way, but were now being influenced by the Pharisees to put sanctification in front of justification.

Now Paul moves to a difficult topic to understand, the penal clause of God's law. God's law has a penal clause contained primarily in Leviticus 26 and Deuteronomy 28. Paul calls the penalties of God's law curses. This penal clause contains over thirty benefits called blessings and over thirty penalties called curses (Lev. 26, Deut. 28). Paul states, "For as many as are of the works of the law are under the curse: for it is written, cursed is every one that **continues not** in all things which are written in the book of the law **to do them**" (Gal. 3:10). Many would say that any who seek to follow God's law are under a curse, but this could not be true. That would be like saying all those who seek to honor their father and mother or refrain from committing adultery will be cursed, but God's law provides a blessing for doing such things. This is demonstrating the same thing as Paul wrote in Romans that "by the deeds of the law there shall no flesh be justified in his sight: **for by the law is the knowledge of sin**." (Rom. 3:20). His conclusion a few verses later was, "For all have sinned, and come short of the glory of God" (Rom. 3:23). Paul is not saying not to keep the law, but not to rely on keeping the law for justification. This is the difference between the "book of the law" and the "curse of the law" (Gal. 3:10).

Paul now contrasts the "book of the law" (Gal. 3:10) with the "curse of the law" (Gal. 3:13). The book of the law contains the commandments, statutes, and judgments of God. The curse of the law contains all the penalties for breaking the book of the law. God's curses/penalties come when we do not continue to practice God's law, but through faith, we have grace to learn God's law. It is important to remember that both parts of God's law are important. The first part, which are the commandments, statutes, and judgments of God, are the perfect standard that God gave for man. As the Messiah stated, "Be therefore perfect, even as your Father which is in heaven is perfect" (Matt. 4:48). The book of the law defines perfection because it is a description of who God is. The second part is the curse of the law, or the penalties of the law. This is necessary because it helps keep man walking in God's ways. In Gal. 3:13 it states, "Christ has redeemed us from the curse of the law, being made a curse for us." Since Christ has become a curse for us, there is now grace to learn how to practice God's law. Since "no man is justified by the law in the sight of God ... The just shall live by faith" (Gal. 3:11). The law will never justify a man, only faith will, for "the law is not of faith" (Gal. 3:12). The flip side to grace/faith is works. As one grows in sanctification they are required to practice more and more of God's law. The writer of Hebrews says, "For if we sin willfully after that we have received the knowledge of the truth, there remains no more sacrifice for sins, but a certain fearful looking for of judgment and fiery indignation, which shall devour the adversaries" (Heb. 10:26-27). This fear of judgment is the curse of the law. If someone knows to follow a certain law, but they do not, the curse/penalty of that law will fall on them, as any loving father would discipline their children.

It is important to remember, God's standard for living is His law. One cannot be saved by the works of the law because, "all have sinned, and come short" (Rom. 3:23) and "whosoever shall keep the whole law, and yet offend in one point, he is guilty of all" (James 2:10). This is why

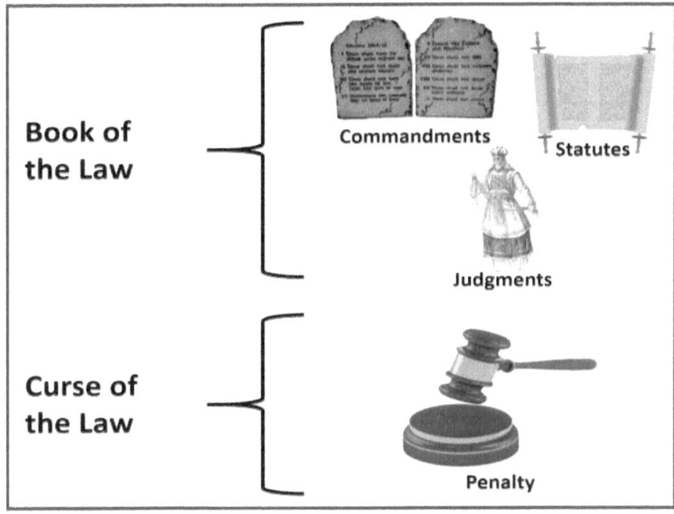

Chart 1. Book of the Law vs Curse of the Law (Israel)

grace is needed. Faith in the Messiah provides the grace needed, but this does not excuse the practice of God's law. Remember, Paul sums up the book of Galatians by saying, "Walk in the Spirit, and you shall not fulfill the lust of the flesh" (Gal. 5:16) and again, "If we live in the Spirit, let us also walk in the Spirit" (Gal. 5:25). But what does it mean to "walk in the spirit?" Ezekiel answers this by quoting God saying, "And I will put my spirit within you, and cause you to walk in my statutes, and you shall keep my judgments, and do them" (Eze. 36:27; Is. 42:4-5). The result of faith in the Messiah is, "that the blessing of Abraham might come on the Gentiles through Jesus Christ" (Gal. 3:14). The blessings of Abraham were from practicing God's law (Gen. 26:4-5). The Messiah was, "made a curse for us" (Gal. 3:13) to give us grace to learn how to follow God's law, but we cannot take advantage of grace by ignoring the practice of God's law.

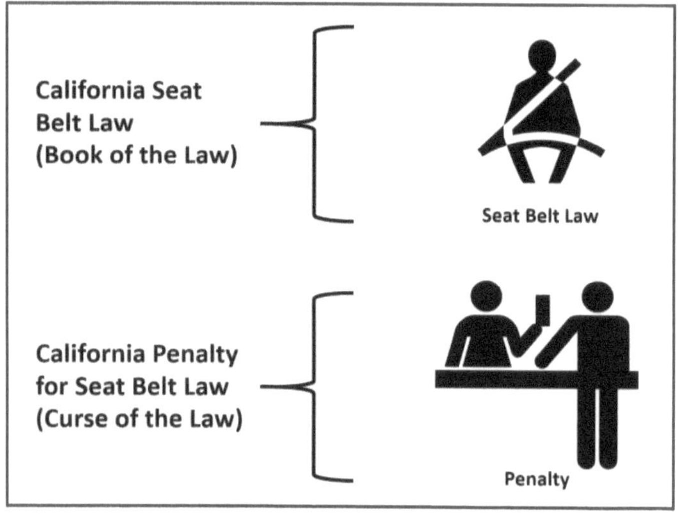

Chart 2. Book of the Law vs Curse of the Law (United States)

Paul now explains the basics of contract (covenant). It is still the same today. "If [a contract/covenant] be confirmed, no man disannuls, or adds thereto" (Gal. 3:15). Once a covenant is made, no one can remove it. God made a contract with Abraham (Gal. 3:16) four hundred and thirty years before the Mosaic Law (Gal. 3:17-18). This contract/promise was to Abraham's "seed" singular, not seeds plural. This contract made to Abraham was the promise of a Messiah. The law cannot "disannul" the promise made over four hundred years earlier. Just as Abraham was saved by grace and received blessings based upon practicing God's law, so are believers today saved by grace and can receive blessings for practicing God's law.

What is the place of the law then? "It was added because of transgressions, till the seed should come to whom the promise was made" (Gal. 3:19). At first glance, it appears the law would only last "till the seed should come," but it is important to remember, there is more than one law in the Old Testament. The context of Galatians 3 is that of comparing the book of the law with the curse of the law. For example, California Vehicle Code has a mandatory seatbelt law (V C Section 27315). There is also another law enforcing this mandatory seatbelt law called a fine and carries a minimum set penalty and court fees. So, there is the first law (mandatory seatbelt law) and the second law (fines) enforcing the first. Scriptural law is the same. There is a law that man is to follow called God's law (book of the law) and there are laws enforcing God's law called the penal clause, or as Paul puts it, curse of the law. The law Paul is saying was "added because of transgressions" is the penal clause to God's law, or curse of the law. The subject matter of the book of Galatians is the "curse of the law" (penal clause) and it is this law that would last "till the seed should come." The only laws that need to be added "because of transgressions" are penalties. There is no need to add more laws. God's law is perfect, but penalties are needed to deal with sin. As already stated, "Christ has redeemed us from the curse/penalty of the law, being made a curse/penalty for us" (Gal. 3:13). He did not redeem us from the book of the law. For those who have faith in the Messiah, the penal clause (curses) are gone because those believers are now under grace to learn to practice God's law. However, as Paul stated in Romans, "Shall we continue in sin, that grace may abound? God forbid. How shall we, that are dead to sin, live any longer therein?" (Rom. 6:1-2) This is a warning to not take advantage of grace. Grace should always lead to an obedient life.

It is also worth noting that a judge can waive the fine, even today, but he cannot repeal the seatbelt law. Someone can pay a fine for someone else, but the law will always remain. God's law is the same. Someone can pay for another's fine (which is what the Messiah did), but God's law will be forever (Deut. 12:28). Those who practice faith in the Messiah need not to fear the curse of the law because through the Holy Spirit they are "walk[ing] in the Spirit" (Gal. 5:16, Eze. 36:27). This in no way implies that the Law of God would end when the Messiah came. The Messiah has become the "curse" of the law, not the law. This only describes the purpose of God's penal clause, until the Messiah came. Once the Messiah came, did He remove the law? On the contrary, the Messiah endorsed the law (Matt. 5:17-18) and He "magnif[ied] the law, and [made] it honorable" (Is. 42:21).

Now the Messiah has become our "mediator" to God (Gal. 3:20). He is our "High Priest" who represents all believers before God (Heb. 2:17). The place of the law was not "against the promises of God," but was to address sin (Gal. 3:21). That is exactly what the law did, it "concluded all under sin, that the promise by faith of Jesus Christ might be given to them that believe" (Gal. 3:22). "But before faith came, we were kept under the law, shut up unto the faith which should afterwards be revealed" (Gal. 3:23). The context here is again the curse/penalties of the law. Before one had faith, they were under the curse of the law, but now after they have faith, they now have grace to learn God's law and follow it (walk in the Spirit - Eze. 36:27). Paul then provides another example of the same thing by stating, "The law was our schoolmaster to bring us unto Christ, that we might be justified by faith" (Gal. 3:24). The Greek word for schoolmaster is παιδαγωγός (paidagōgos) which means "a boy leader, that is, a servant whose office it was to take the children to school."[54] This word referred not to a teacher or tutor, but to an office given to "slaves or freedmen" whose main duty was to "watch over the boys; to restrain them from evil and temptation; and to conduct them to the schools"[55] The Schoolmaster was "one who was entrusted with the supervision of a family, taking them to and from the school, being responsible for their safety and manners. **Hence the pedagogue was stern and severe in his discipline**."[56] The main duty of the "schoolmaster" was that of disciplining the children in their care, just as the law's main duty was to discipline God's people with curses/penalties. God's law disciplines men with blessing and curses to bring them to the Messiah. This is echoed in Heb. 12:6-8 where the writer quotes Prov. 3:12 saying, "For whom the Lord loves he chastens, and scourges every son whom he receives." God's law disciplines man to bring

---

[54] Strong, James, "Schoolmaster - paidagōgos." *A Concise Dictionary of the Words in the Greek Bible*, pg. 54, G3807.

[55] Albert Barnes, *Barnes New Testament Notes*, Gal. 3:24, Grand Rapids, Michigan. Baker Book House, 1949.

[56] M.G. Easton, M.A., D.D., *Easton's Bible Dictionary*, Third Edition, Gal. 3:24, Thomas Nelson, 1897.

them to the Messiah to receive forgiveness. Those who practice faith in the Messiah can expect discipline (curses) if, or when, they sin, which is breaking God's law (1 John 3:4).

Paul concludes by showing the difference when someone has faith in the Messiah. "But after that faith is come, we are no longer under a schoolmaster. For you are all the children of God by faith in Christ Jesus" (Gal. 3:25-27). After one puts their faith in the Messiah, they become sons and no longer need discipline to keep them following God's law. They are now walking in the Spirit, which is "walk[ing] in [God's] statutes, and keep[ing His] judgments, and do[ing] them" (Eze. 36:27). This is no different than a good father disciplining his children. A child will do what is right out of fear of the consequences from their father. When that child matures they will start doing what is right because they now know why it is right. They have truly become a child of their father because they follow his will willingly. Currently, there is no longer a need for consequences. The same is true for the believer. Once they place their faith in the Messiah of Israel, they now desire to be obedient to the Heavenly Father through the Messiah. Now, there is no longer any need for the schoolmaster to discipline. There is no longer any need for the curse of the law because willing obedience has been obtained.

Paul continues, "there is neither Jew nor Greek, there is neither bond nor free, there is neither male nor female: for you are all one in Christ Jesus" (Gal. 3:28). Faith in the Messiah has made a way for Gentiles to join covenant with God. As Paul said in Ephesians, the Messiah made "in himself of two one new man, so making peace" (Eph. 2:15). The Gentiles are now able to be grafted in through faith in the Messiah (Rom. 11:17). Paul concludes this chapter with, "And if you are Messiah's, then you are Abraham's seed, and heirs according to the promise" (Gal. 3:29). The promise of God is faith in the Messiah of Israel to forgive the sins of all those who have faith in Him. This does not remove the law, for the law is for our benefit. What it does do is provide grace to learn how to "walk in the Spirit" (practice God's law), so not to "fulfill the lust of the flesh" (Gal. 5:16). Walking in the Spirit is the same as walking in the commandments of God (Eze. 36:27).

It is very unfortunate that this chapter is often used to say God's law is not for today. Almost all law works the same. There is first a law that is written, and then there is a secondary law called a penal clause that is designed to enforce the first law. Biblical law is the same even if it uses different terms. There is first a law that is written in the book of the law, then there is secondary law written in the curse of the law that is designed to enforce the first law. When God's law is looked at from a legal perspective it is clear that Galatians in no way removes God's law (book of the law), but faith can remove the penalties of God's law (curse of the law). The curse of the law (penalties) can be removed, but the book of the law (God's law) is forever. The Messiah can and has removed the penalties for those who put their faith in him. This is exactly what Paul said, the "Messiah has redeemed us from the curse of the law, being made a curse for us (Gal. 3:13)."

The Handwriting of Ordinances (Col. 2):

Colossians 2 is probably the most common chapter people use to say that the Law of God is abolished. In fact, the verse in question when taken by itself does sound like this is what it is saying. However, a simple study of the context around it will dispel this myth. Here is the entire passage from Colossians 2.

> Beware lest any man spoil you through philosophy and vain deceit, after the tradition of men, after the rudiments of the world, and not after Christ. For in him dwells all the fulness of the Godhead bodily. And you are complete in him, which is the head of all principality and power: In whom also you are circumcised with the circumcision made without hands, in putting off the body of the sins of the flesh by the circumcision of Christ: Buried with him in baptism, wherein also you are risen with him through the faith of the operation of God, who has raised him from the dead. And you, being dead in your sins and the uncircumcision of your flesh, has he quickened together with him, having forgiven you all trespasses; **Blotting out the handwriting of ordinances that was against us, which was contrary to us, and took it out of the way, nailing it to his cross**; And having spoiled principalities and powers, he made a show of them openly, triumphing over them in it. Let no man therefore judge you in meat, or in drink, or in respect of a holyday, or of the new moon, or of the sabbath days: which are a shadow of things to come; but the body is of Christ. Let no man beguile you of your reward in a voluntary humility and worshipping of angels, intruding into those things which he has not seen, vainly puffed up by his

> fleshly mind, and not holding the Head, from which all the body by joints and bands having nourishment ministered, and knit together, increases with the increase of God. Wherefore if you are dead with Christ from the rudiments of the world, why, as though living in the world, are you subject to ordinances, (Touch not; taste not; handle not; Which all are to perish with the using;) after the commandments and doctrines of men? (Col. 2:8-22)

The key verse used is, "Blotting out the handwriting of ordinances that was against us, which was contrary to us, and took it out of the way, **nailing it to his cross**" (Col. 2:14). Many believers today will say, "the Law of God was nailed to the cross with Jesus." As will be seen, through careful study, this passage teaches no such thing. The topic for this passage starts in verse eight where the Apostle Paul states the purpose of this portion of Scripture. Paul starts off with a warning to, "Beware lest any man spoil you through **philosophy** and **vain deceit**, after the **tradition of men**, after the **rudiments of the world**, and not after Christ" (Col. 2:8). It is important to remember that the remainder of the chapter is dealing with "philosophy," "vain deceit," "the tradition of men," and "the rudiments of the world." Understanding this will make it easier to understand what Paul is trying to say.

In the next four verses Paul explains the position of the believer in Christ. The Colossians are "complete in Him" (Col. 2:10), of "the circumcision made without hands" (Col. 2:11), are "buried with him in baptism" (Col. 2:12), and are "dead in [their] sins" and have been "forgiven ... all [their] trespasses" (Col. 2:13). Clearly the believer has been restored before God for they are "complete in Him" and need nothing from man to add to what God has done. The next verse, however, is the verse commonly quoted to show how God's law has been abolished.

In Colossians 2:14, Paul states that the Messiah, "Blott[ed] out the handwriting of ordinances that was against us, which was contrary to us, and took it out of the way, nailing it to his cross." Many take this verse off point and out of context to make their case that the Law of God is done away with, but this is simply not true. It is needful to understand what, "the handwriting of ordinances" were. The Greek word for ordinance is dogma which means, "a law (civil, ceremonial or ecclesiastical): - decree or ordinance."[57] Does this mean that Paul is speaking of the Law of God? If the subject is still "vain deceit," "the tradition of men," and "the rudiments of the world," then it is highly doubtful that he is speaking of God's law. The ordinances referred to here are the religious dogma of the Pharisees. The Pharisees were a group who sought to judge others by their own tradition and added to God's law (Matt. 12:2, Matt 15:1-3, Matt. 16:11-12). Their tradition is what was against us. The Messiah has removed these for us. In fact, the Greek word dogma appears five times in the New Testament (Luke 2:1, Acts 16:4, Acts 17:7, Eph. 2:15, Col. 2:14). The first three are clearly referring to an ordinance of man. In both Ephesians and Colossians, it is commonly assumed that this word refers to the Law of God, nevertheless, with proper study it will become clear that the word dogma always refers to man's

---

[57] Strong, James, "Ordinance - dogma." *A Concise Dictionary of the Words in the Greek Bible*, pg. 24, G1378.

ordinances/statutes and never to God's law. To further support this we can simply turn to the Septuagint Old Testament. The word dogma is used fourteen times in the Septuagint Old Testament. Each time it is referencing a statute from man. Never does it refer to the Law of God. The ordinances here in Colossians are the tradition of the Elders the Messiah dealt with throughout the Gospels. This will become clearer in the next few verses.

In Colossians 2:15, Paul continues stating that the Messiah "spoiled principalities and powers," and he "made a show of them openly, triumphing over them in it." An obvious question to this statement is, when did the Messiah do this? The Greek word for principalities is archē which means "chief (in various applications of order, time, place or rank)."[58] The Greek word for powers is, exousia which means, "concretely magistrate, superhuman, potentate, token of control."[59] Both these words refer to someone in authority, but who did the Messiah "make a show of ... openly" and was in authority? As always, the Scripture has the answer. In Matt. 5:20, Matt. 9:3-4, Matt. 15:1-9, Matt. 23:26-33, Mark 12:35-37, Mark 12:38-40, Luke 18:10-14 and many more, the Messiah openly and publicly challenged the Jewish leaders (Scribes and Pharisees). In fact, many of his conversations with them could be described as harsh and severe. The Scribes and Pharisees are the principalities and powers mentioned in Colossians 2. This fits well because both archē and exousia are used for various rulers and leaders, including the rulers

---

[58] Strong, James, "Principalities - archē." *A Concise Dictionary of the Words in the Greek Bible*, pg. 16, G746.

[59] Strong, James, "Powers - exousia." *A Concise Dictionary of the Words in the Greek Bible*, pg. 30, G1849.

and leaders of the Jews (Luke 23:7, Acts 9:14, Acts 26:10, etc.). Furthermore, several well-known commentators make this conclusion. Adam Clark says,

> And the principalities and powers refer to the emperors, kings, and generals taken in battle, and reserved to grace the victor's triumph. It is very likely that by the αρχας και εξουσιας, principalities and powers, over whom Christ triumphed, the apostle means the נשיאות nesioth and רשות roshoth, who were the rulers and chiefs in the Sanhedrin and synagogues, and who had great authority among the people, both in making constitutions and explaining traditions.[60]

Though these two Greek words sometimes refer to spiritual rulers, the phrase used is most common for rulers taken in battle, and so it most likely refers to the physical rulers of the Jews. This matches the previous verses where Paul called them, "philosophy," "vain deceit," "the tradition of men," and "the rudiments of the world." The "ordinances", or "dogma" that Paul is speaking of is the tradition of the elders that the Pharisees put on the people. This will be seen even more clearly as we continue.

"Let no man therefore judge you in meat, or in drink, or in respect of a holyday, or of the new moon, or of the Sabbath days" (Col. 2:16). These are the holy days of God, not of the world (Lev. 23:2). This passage is not saying that the Colossians should not practice these holy days, but that they should not let anyone judge them as they learn

---

[60] Clark, Adam, *Clarks's Commentary*, NT, Vol 6A, Romans – Colossians PDF, pg. 1162.

how to practice them. This was the tradition of the Scribes and Pharisees. They added ordinances and statutes to God's law (judging them) to restrict the people of God as to how to follow God's law. These are the fence laws mentioned earlier. It is important to remember that the believers in Colossae were Gentile believers. As a result, you can presume that they had little experience practicing God's law. This is where grace comes into play. God is extending grace to all those who have faith in the Messiah to learn and practice His law. As one learns more and more what God's word has to say and how to apply it to his/her life, one needs grace. This is evidenced by some of the other epistles Paul wrote. After all, he was the, "apostle of the Gentiles" (Rom. 11:13). In 1 Cor. 5:7-8, Paul, when speaking of the feast of Passover, instructs the Gentile Corinthians to "keep the feast." Since the Corinthians wrote to Paul asking questions in a previous letter (1 Cor. 7:1), then it is safe to assume that among these were questions regarding Passover which is why he answered as he did.

Why should believers practice these holy days? The answer is simple, they are a "shadow of things to come" (Col. 2:17). Like a shadow that is seen first, each one of these holy days predicts an aspect of future events. The spring feasts foreshadow the Messiah's first coming, and the fall feasts foreshadow his second coming. See Table 4.

YHVH's Holy Days		
First Coming	•	The Passover foreshadows the Messiah's sacrificial death.
	•	First fruits foreshadow the Messiah's resurrection.
	•	The Days of Unleavened Bread foreshadows man's sanctification.
	•	The Feast of Weeks (Pentecost) foreshadows the giving of the Holy Spirit.
Second Coming	•	The Day of Trumpets foreshadows the second coming of the Messiah.
	•	The Day of Atonement foreshadows the judgment of the nations.
	•	The Feast of Tabernacles foreshadows the millennial reign of the Messiah.
	•	The Eighth Day foreshadows the new beginning and eternity.

Table 4

It stands to reason that since there are feasts yet to be fulfilled at the second coming of the Messiah, the church today should at least practice those feasts. This writer believes that all of God's holy days should still be kept today. Remember, according to Psalms 111:10, "a good understanding have all they that do his commandments." If believers want to understand the events foreshadowed by these feasts, then believers need to practice these feasts. In fact, there is a word associated with God's holy days. This word is the Hebrew word מִקְרָא (miqrā') and means, "something called out, i.e. a public meeting; also a rehearsal."[61] These holy days are rehearsals. This is what the Apostle Paul is speaking of. Keeping these rehearsals teaches God's plan to His people. When they are not kept, there is significantly less understanding of them. For

---

[61] Strong, James, "Holy Convocation – מִקְרָא miqrā'." *A Concise Dictionary of the Words in the Hebrew Bible*, pg. 71, H4744.

believers to understand the plan set forth in God's holy days they need to rehearse them yearly.

Furthermore, in verse seventeen, it should be noted that it is the same sentence as verse sixteen. The phrase "which are a shadow of things to come," is a context clue before the conclusion of the sentence. The conclusion of the sentence is, "But the body *is* of Christ." The word "is" is not in the original text, which is why the King James translation has it in italics. If the context clue and the word "is" are removed, then the sentence becomes clear. Believers are to, "Let no man therefore judge [them] in meat, or in drink, or in respect of a holyday, or of the new moon, or of the Sabbath days, ... but the body of Christ." Only the body of Christ should judge or determine how believers are to practice these holy days. This thought is echoed in 1 Cor. 5:12-13 where Paul says, "For what have I to do to judge them also that are without? do not ye judge them that are within? But them that are without God judges." Members of the body of Christ are to judge themselves in an attempt to follow God's law and incorporate it into their lives. They are not to let the dogma of the Pharisees judge or cause them to feel bad for keeping these feasts. Fortunately, God shows grace for those who want to learn God's commandments.

Verses eighteen and nineteen are repeating what was said in verses eight and nine. They are not to allow anyone to "beguile [them] of [their] reward" by convincing them to "worship angels ... which [they] have not seen." This causes them to be "puffed up in [their] fleshly mind" (Col. 2:18-19). Since they are, "dead with Christ from the rudiments of the world, why, as though living in the world, are you subject to ordinances," (Col. 2:20). This is more evidence that Paul is speaking about worldly ordinances, and not God's law. In fact, the next verse demonstrates the mind of the Pharisees when challenging the Messiah by saying, "Touch not; taste not; handle not" (Col. 2:21). This was a mantra of the leaders of the Jews. According to John Gill, the Apostle Paul is speaking, "but in the person of the Jewish doctors; who [were] urging the use of the ceremonial law." [62] The ceremonial laws were the laws added to God's law. These are the fence laws of the Pharisees. They were to "touch not" the dead body of any man "taste not" a gnat that accidentally flew into their mouth (Matt. 23:24), and "handle not" anything unclean. All of this is a distortion of God's law and follows after the tradition of men. In fact, the next thing that Paul states is that this is all going to perish "after the **commandments and doctrines of men.**" The answer here is clearly given. Paul is clearly talking about the commandments and doctrines of men, not God. This is exactly the problem the Messiah faced when He walked the earth. Over and over the Messiah challenged the religious leaders and their traditions (Matt. 15:2-3, Mark 7:3-13). In fact, when the entire passage is looked at as a whole, it becomes clear that the beginning and ending of this entire passage refers to "philosophy," "vain deceit," the "tradition of men," the "rudiments of the world," the "rudiments of the world" a second time, and the "commandments and doctrines of men." The verse in question is surrounded by the phrases

---

[62] Gill, John, *John Gill's Exposition of the Bible*, Colossians 2:21, Obtained July 31, 2024, https://sacred-texts.com/bib/cmt/gill/col002.htm.

that prove Paul is speaking of the tradition of the elders as can clearly be seen below.

> Beware lest any man spoil you through **philosophy** and **vain deceit**, after the **tradition of men**, after the **rudiments of the world**, and not after Christ. For in him dwells all the fulness of the Godhead bodily. And you are complete in him, which is the head of all principality and power: In whom also you are circumcised with the circumcision made without hands, in putting off the body of the sins of the flesh by the circumcision of Christ: Buried with him in baptism, wherein also you are risen with him through the faith of the operation of God, who has raised him from the dead. And you, being dead in your sins and the uncircumcision of your flesh, has he quickened together with him, having forgiven you all trespasses; **Blotting out the handwriting of ordinances that was against us, which was contrary to us, and took it out of the way, nailing it to his cross**; And having spoiled principalities and powers, he made a shew of them openly, triumphing over them in it. Let no man therefore judge you in meat, or in drink, or in respect of a holyday, or of the new moon, or of the sabbath days: Which are a shadow of things to come; but the body is of Christ. Let no man beguile you of your reward in a voluntary humility and worshipping of angels, intruding into those things which he has not seen, vainly puffed up by his fleshly mind, And not holding the Head, from which all the body by joints and bands having nourishment ministered, and knit together, increases with the increase of God. Wherefore if you be dead with Christ from the **rudiments of the world**, why, as though living in the world, are you

> subject to ordinances, (Touch not; taste not; handle not; Which all are to perish with the using;) **after the commandments and doctrines of men**?

In summary, it is clear from the text, that Colossians 2 in no way removes the Law of God, nor "nails it to the cross." What is nailed to the cross is the tradition of the elders that were adding to God's Word. Paul starts in verse eight warning us not to follow after the "traditions of men" (Col. 2:8). These traditions come from the religious leaders of the day known as the Scribes and Pharisees. They had numerous writings adding statutes and regulations to God's law. Their writings are preserved today in a collection called the Talmud. It is these types of extra-biblical writings that believers should be aware of. The appeal here is to stick to the Scripture and not to add to or take away from God's law (Deut. 4:2, Deut. 12:32). Paul even ends this passage the way he began, with an appeal to beware of, "the commandments and doctrines of men" (Col. 2:22). As the Messiah stated, "Till heaven and earth pass, one jot or one tittle shall in no wise pass from the law, till all be fulfilled" (Matt. 5:18). If there is an earth beneath and a sky above, all of God's law still remains. The amazing thing is, God offers grace to all those who practice faith in the Messiah so that they might learn how to practice His law.

Commandments Contained in Ordinances (Eph. 2):

Ephesians 2 is another chapter similar to Colossians 2. The same word is used and is translated as "ordinances." The most common interpretation is that the Apostle Paul is referring to God's law and not man's law. However, it is easily demonstrated that this is not the case. Here is the passage in its entirety.

> And you has he quickened, who were dead in trespasses and sins; Wherein in time past you walked according to the course of this world, according to the prince of the power of the air, the spirit that now works in the children of disobedience: Among whom also we all had our conversation in times past in the lusts of our flesh, fulfilling the desires of the flesh and of the mind; and were by nature the children of wrath, even as others. But God, who is rich in mercy, for his great love wherewith he loved us, even when we were dead in sins, has quickened us together with Christ, (by grace you are saved;) And has raised us up together, and made us sit together in heavenly places in Christ Jesus: That in the ages to come he might shew the exceeding riches of his grace in his kindness toward us through Christ Jesus. For by grace are you saved through faith; and that not of yourselves: it is the gift of God: Not of works, lest any man should boast. For we are his workmanship, created in Christ Jesus unto good works, which God has before ordained that we should walk in them. Wherefore remember, that you being in time past Gentiles in the flesh, who are called Uncircumcision by that which is called the Circumcision in the flesh made by hands; That at that time you were without Christ, being aliens from the commonwealth of Israel, and strangers from the covenants of promise, having no hope, and without God in the world: But now in Christ Jesus you who sometimes were far off are made nigh by the blood of Christ. For he is our peace, who has made both one, and has broken down the

middle wall of partition between us; **Having abolished in his flesh the enmity, even the law of commandments contained in ordinances**; for to make in himself of two one new man, so making peace; and that he might reconcile both unto God in one body by the cross, having slain the enmity thereby: and came and preached peace to you which were afar off, and to them that were nigh. For through him we both have access by one Spirit unto the Father. Now therefore you are no more strangers and foreigners, but fellow citizens with the saints, and of the household of God; and are built upon the foundation of the apostles and prophets, Jesus Christ himself being the chief corner stone; In whom all the building fitly framed together grows unto a holy temple in the Lord: In whom you also are built together for a habitation of God through the Spirit. (Eph. 2:1-22)

The verse in question is Eph. 2:15. This verse says, "Having abolished in his flesh the enmity, even the law of commandments contained in ordinances; for to make in himself of two one new man, so making peace" (Eph. 2:15). The word for ordinances is the same word for ordinances in Colossians 2:14. This word is dogma and means, "law (civil, ceremonial or ecclesiastical): - decree or ordinance."[63] In both the New Testament and the Septuagint Old Testament this word is always used to reference secular law. The only exception to that seems to be Colossians 2 and Ephesians 2. It has already been demonstrated that in Colossians 2 this word does not

---

[63] Strong, James, "Ordinance - dogma." *A Concise Dictionary of the Words in the Greek Bible*, pg. 24, G1378.

represent God's law, but rather represents man's law, but what about Ephesians 2?

The chapter starts with a reminder to the Gentiles of where they came from. They were "dead in trespasses and sins" (Eph. 2:1), they "walked according to the course of this world" (Eph. 2:2), and they "were by nature the children of wrath" (Eph. 2:3). "But God, who is rich in mercy," (Eph. 2:4) changed this while they were "dead in sins", and He "quickened [them] together with Christ" (Eph. 2:5). God did this to show "the exceeding riches of his grace" (Eph. 2:7). The Ephesians are reminded of where they came from and the great gift God has given them.

This all leads to one of the most popular verses in all of Scripture. "For by grace are you saved through faith; and that not of yourselves: it is the gift of God: Not of works, lest any man should boast" (Eph. 2:8-9). They are saved by grace through faith apart from any works they can do. This is their justification where God forgives them of all their sins, but the next verse explains their sanctification where they are to work with God to become the person He wants them to be. "For we are his workmanship, created in Christ Jesus unto good works, which God has before ordained that we should walk in them" (Eph. 2:10). It is important to point out the contrast between verse two and verse ten. In verse two, Paul describes how they "walked according to the course of this world" and in verse ten Paul explains how God had "ordained that we should walk." The question might be asked, where did God ordain how they should walk? Afterall, this is past tense. They are God's "workmanship," "created in the Messiah unto good works," that, "God has before ordained." When did God before ordain their good works? The answer is in Exodus 16:4, where God clearly states that they should "walk in [His] law." This is echoed over and over throughout the Old Testament as well (see Lev. 26:3, Deut. 26:17, Deut. 30:16, 1 Kings 2:3, 1 Kings 6:12, Neh. 10:29, Psalm 119:1, and many more). The point here is that God told them how to walk, but they didn't. In the Old Testament, the prophets continually told the people of God to repent and turn back to following God's law (Dan. 9:10, Neh. 10:29), and in the New Testament the Messiah and the apostles are doing the same (Matt. 5:17-19, Rom. 2:13). Fortunately, God has offered forgiveness that He might work with believers to bring them back to walking in God's law. The good works that believers were created for in the Messiah is the Law of God.

In verse eleven, Paul moves on to another aspect of this work, the Jew and Gentile division. In the past, they were called "Gentiles in the flesh" and "Uncircumcision" by the "Circumcision in the flesh made by hands," or by the Jews (Eph. 2:11). The Jews segregated from the Gentiles which caused the Gentiles to be "aliens from the commonwealth of Israel" and "strangers from the covenants of promise" (Eph. 2:12). But now they "are made nigh by the blood of Christ" (Eph. 2:13) who has, "broken down the middle wall of partition between [them]" (Eph. 2:14). This "middle wall" was a division in the temple where the court of the Gentiles was separated from the Jews. Josephus said it this way, "The middle was much higher than the rest . . . In the midst of which, and not far from it, was the second, to be gone up to by a few steps: this was encompassed by a stone wall for a partition, with an inscription, which forbade any foreigner to go in under pain of death."[64] The Jewish extra-biblical laws, most of which are contained in the writing today called the Talmud, had many laws that require segregation from the Gentiles. These laws are not found in the Scripture. For example, in the Talmud a Jew does not have to pay a Gentile his wages (Sanhedrin 57a), a Jew has superior legal rights (Baba Kamma 37b), and a Jew may lie to a Gentile to gain financial advantage (Baba Kamma 113a). These principles are found nowhere in Scripture. The Scripture does have laws concerning "strangers," but these laws are different. If a stranger lives in the land, then they are to keep God's laws and be treated as brethren (Ex. 12:49, Ex. 22:21, Ex. 23:9). God does show a distinction between those who practice His laws and those who don't, but this is not based upon race, it is based upon the practice of His Laws.

The Middle Wall of Partition, Holyland Model of Jerusalem, Berthold Werner

---

[64] Josephus, Flavius. *The Works of Flavius Josephus*. Translated into English, by William Whiston, The Antiquities of the Jews, Book 15, chapter 11, par. 416-417.

It is important to identify what the commonwealth of Israel is. The Greek word for commonwealth is politeia, which means, "citizenship; concretely a community."[65] These Gentiles were excommunicated from having citizenship in the Kingdom of Israel (God's Kingdom). Remember, a stranger, or alien, was always allowed to become part of the Kingdom of Israel, but they had to practice God's law (Ex. 12:49, Ex. 22:21, Ex. 23:9). Unfortunately, the Jews were keeping Gentiles away which is contrary to God's law. This is what the middle wall of partition was. The Scribes and Pharisees were adding to and taking away from God's law (Deut. 4:2). This was done with bias and prejudice to keep the Gentiles away from the promises of God. Paul is not stating anything new, but putting things back to the way they should be. When believers put their faith in the Messiah, they are changing their citizenship to the Kingdom of Heaven/Israel. This is important. If someone were to change citizenships from the United States to Australia, wouldn't they stop practicing the law of the United States and start practicing the law of Australia? The same is true for believers in their salvation. When believers put their faith in the Messiah, they are to stop practicing the "law of sin" (Rom. 8:2) and start practicing the Law of God. This is why believers are called "ambassadors" (2 Cor. 5:20, Eph. 6:20). This is a legal term. An ambassador lives in a foreign land, but practices the law of their homeland. The ambassador for the United States might live in Australia, but he practices the law of the United States. Believers do the same. They live on this earth, but they practice the law of their

---

[65] Strong, James, "Commonwealth - politeia." *A Concise Dictionary of the Words in the Greek Bible*, pg. 59, G4174.

homeland (Law of God). This is what makes them a "peculiar people" (1 Pet. 2:9).

This is the background that leads up to the verse in question. "Having abolished in his flesh the enmity, even the law of commandments contained in ordinances; for to make in himself of two one new man, so making peace" (Eph. 2:15). The Messiah abolished the enmity (echthra - hostility)[66], which is the "law of commandments contained in ordinances." The Greek word for ordinances is dogma which means, "a law (civil, ceremonial or ecclesiastical): - decree, ordinance."[67] This is the same word from Colossians 2. As stated before, this word appears in the New Testament five times, three times it is translated as decree and two times as ordinance. In every instance it refers to a law of man (Luke 2:1, Acts 16:4, Acts 17:7, Eph. 2:15, Col. 2:14). This word also appears in the Septuagint Old Testament fourteen times. Each time it refers to a law of man. Paul is speaking of the religious dogma of the Scribes and Pharisees as recorded in the Talmud, which is contrary to God's law. This passage of Scripture in no way endorses the abolishment of God's law, rather it upholds God's law by supporting the statute that states not to add to or take away from God's law (Deut. 4:2, Deut. 12:32). The Jews added statute upon statute to God's law which oppressed the Jewish people, as well as the Gentiles. It is this burdensome law that was abolished. The end result is

---

[66] Strong, James, "Enmity - echthra." *A Concise Dictionary of the Words in the Greek Bible*, pg. 34, G2189.

[67] Strong, James, "Ordinance - dogma." *A Concise Dictionary of the Words in the Greek Bible*, pg. 24, G1378.

that both Jew and Gentile are "reconcile[d] ... unto God in one body by the cross" (Eph. 2:16).

As stated in the analysis of Colossians, these ordinances that Paul is speaking of are mentioned over and over in the gospels. The Messiah himself constantly had to deal with these extra-biblical laws. Remember, the Messiah was constantly being accused of breaking God's law, but this could not have been true or he could not be the Messiah. In Deuteronomy 13, God warned about following false prophets who speak "to turn you away from YHVH your God" and "thrust you out of the way which YHVH your God commanded you to walk in" (Deut. 13:5). Yeshua/Jesus could not have been the Messiah unless he followed and endorsed every commandment of God. The reality was that the Jews were accusing the Messiah not of breaking God's law, but of breaking the "tradition of the elders" (Matt. 15:2-3). The Law of God is "holy, and just, and good" (Rom. 7:12), but the "tradition of the elders" adds to and takes away from God's law. The "tradition of the elders" makes God's law of "none effect" (Matt. 15:6). This law is oppressive and divisive and not according to God's will.

This passage is concluded by demonstrating the result of the Messiah's work. The Messiah "preached peace to [them] which were afar off" (Eph. 2:17). So, now both Jew and Gentile "have access by one Spirit unto the Father" (Eph. 2:18). They are, "no more strangers and foreigners, but fellow citizens with the saints, and of the household of God. Built upon the foundation of the apostles and prophets, the Messiah himself being the chief corner stone" (Eph. 2:19-20). This concludes the previous thought. The Gentiles were once alienated from citizenship, but now they are "fellow citizens." This alienation came from man (Scribes and Pharisees) and not from God. The Messiah is building a new temple which contains both Jew and Gentile, as a "habitation of God through the Spirit" (Eph. 2:21-22). This is echoed by Paul in 1 Cor. 6:19 where he said, "know you not that your body is the temple of the Holy Ghost which is in you, which you have of God, and you are not your own?" The word for "your" is ὑμῶν (humōn). This word is plural. The body that is referred to here as the Temple is plural. This is referring to the church's body of believers. The church is now the Temple of God, and the Messiah is building this temple now through our justification and sanctification.

The Messiah has accomplished a tremendous amount by his work on the cross, but he did not abolish God's law. The Messiah abolished man's laws of division and racism and brought all who have faith in the Messiah of Israel together. God's law is good for man. His health laws keep them healthy, His financial laws keep them financially stable, and His government laws keep them holy. Why would they not want to follow His laws? It is very unfortunate that the church today interprets passages like this to remove a law that is such a blessing for God's people.

In summary, there are many other verses in the Scripture that are commonly used to say God's law is no longer relevant today. The truth is, through proper study, these verses say no such thing. In fact, many times they actually end up endorsing the Law of God. The question of relevance is very unfortunate because God's law is "holy, and the commandment holy, and just, and good" (Rom. 7:12). Not practicing God's law can actually do man harm. Believers should always properly understand God's law with God's intended purpose. This is what the spirit of the law is. Understanding God's law with His intent in mind. When this is done, it quickly becomes clear that God's law is not for justification, but rather for sanctification. God provides justification by faith in the Messiah, which is the covenant of promise He made to Abraham. God's law does not save man, but man practices God's law because they are so grateful for the salvation they have freely received. Faith is the root of salvation, but obedience is the fruit of salvation. To better understand this, it is important to understand the meaning of covenant in light of love and faith.

Chapter Six

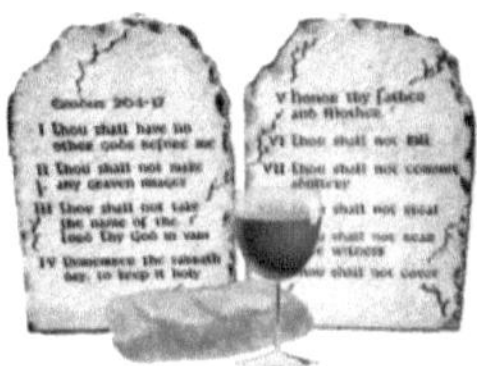

Love, Faith, and Covenant

Throughout history, God has made covenants with man. Understanding these covenants is critical to understanding the purpose God has throughout history. These covenants cannot be understood without first understanding the biblical definitions of love, faith, and covenant. These three words have a different meaning in the Scripture than what most believe. You cannot understand one without the other. Probably the most misunderstood of these words is the word for love. Many believers talk about the love of God. It is a common theme in many circles of conversation within Christianity, even amongst unbelievers. Throughout the Scripture, we hear about the amazing love of God, but many times we do not take the time to really understand what this word means. This chapter will discuss these terms from a scriptural perspective.

What is Biblical Love?

It is commonly taught that there are two types of love in the Bible, phileo love and agape love. Phileo love is taught to be a brotherly love one has towards another, but agape love is taught to be an unconditional divine love from God. The confusion we have today is with agape love. The most common definition of agape love is an unconditional divine love from God. This is an unfortunate definition because the true definition of agape is not a divine love at all. If it was a divine love, then how could it be used in a love towards evil? In John 3:19, the Messiah said that, "Men loved (agape) darkness rather than light, because their deeds were evil." This is right after he said, "For God so loved (agape) the world, that he gave his only begotten Son, that whosoever believes in him should not perish, but have everlasting life" (John 3:16). How could agape possibly mean divine love from God when men use it to love darkness? Agape is also not unconditional. If agape love was unconditional, God could never stop loving man, but He clearly says he "hates all workers of iniquity" (Psalms 5:5). How can God love someone unconditionally, then hate them later for their iniquity? This is not unconditional. The fact is that agape love is not divine love or unconditional love, but something entirely different.

The word ἀγάπη/agape means "love, that is, affection or benevolence."[68] This, however, is an oversimplification of the word and not a good definition. A more thorough definition is "love, affectionate regard, goodwill, benevolence. With reference to God's love, it is God's

---

[68] Strong, James, "Love - agapē." *A Concise Dictionary of the Words in the Greek Bible*, pg. 7, G26.

willful direction toward man. It involves God doing what He knows is best for man and not necessarily what man desires."[69] This definition changes what agape means. It is not just an affectionate feeling towards someone, but involves a thought-out plan of affection. Professor William Barclay adds to this understanding in his book *New Testament Words* when he said,

> Agape has to do with the mind: it is not simply an emotion which rises unbidden in our hearts; it is a principle by which we deliberately live. Agape has supremely to do with the will. It is a conquest, a victory, and achievement. No one ever naturally loved his enemies. To love one's enemies is a conquest of all our natural inclinations and emotions.[70]

Agape is not based on a feeling. Feelings arrive passively based upon our own emotions. Agape must be cultivated; it is a choice. Feelings are triggered by external events such as the weather, people's actions, or internal processes such as digestion or thought. Liking is a feeling, but agape is a commitment, independent of our likes and dislikes. People are not responsible for their feelings because they can't help how they feel, but they are responsible for their agape because agape is an act of will. Barclay continues by saying,

> [Agape] is not simply a wave of emotion; it is a deliberate conviction of the mind issuing in a deliberate policy of the life; it is a deliberate

---

[69] Zodhiates, Spiros Th.D., "Love - agapē." *The Complete Word Study Dictionary*, pg. 66, G26.

[70] Barclay, William, *New Testament Words*, (Louisville Kentucky, Westminster John Knox Press, 1974), 21.

> achievement and conquest and victory of the will. It takes all of a man to achieve Christian love; it takes not only his heart; it takes his mind and his will as well.[71]

This is a very different understanding of agape than simple affection toward another. To put this in modern terms, agape love is what might be called today "tough love." It is a love that causes someone to do what is right even when what is right is very difficult to do. Parents need to demonstrate this tough love, or agape love, when disciplining their children. It is not easy to spank a child when needed, but it does show agape love when done properly. Agape is a purposeful, thought-out plan and a course of action. As Paul said to the Corinthians, love is long suffering, kind, not envious, not proud or arrogant, not rude, does not seek its own, not easily angered, does not think evil, is not happy with sin, but loves the truth (1 Cor. 13:4-6).

Although 1 Corinthians 13 describes love, this is not the definition of love. The Scriptures are clear in the definition of key words. There is always a verse that provides the definition, it just needs to be searched for. In 1 John 5:2-3, the Apostle John states, "By this we know that we love (agapaō) the children of God, when we love (agapaō) God, and keep his commandments. For this is the love (agape) of God, **that we keep his commandments**: and his commandments are not grievous." This is echoed in other passages as well. In fact, when a search for love in the Scripture is done, it would surprise many how often

---

[71] Barclay, William, *New Testament Words*, (Louisville Kentucky, Westminster John Knox Press, 1974), 22.

love is compared to God's law. You can't have one without the other. In John 14:15, the Messiah states, "If you love (agapaō) me, keep my commandments." The Messiah repeated this again in John 15:9-10 when He said, "As the Father has loved (agapaō) me, so have I loved (agapaō) you: continue in my love (agapē). If you keep my commandments, you shall abide in my love (agapē); even as I have kept my Father's commandments, and abide in his love (agapē)." It seems clear that the Messiah understood love as when someone keeps the commandments of God. In fact, a proper study of God's law will reveal the same. In Ex. 20:6, God said He shows "mercy unto thousands of them that love [Him], and keep [His] commandments." This is repeated in Deut. 30:16, " . . . I command you this day to love YHVH your God, to walk in his ways, and to keep his commandments and his statutes and his judgments." Over and over in the Old Testament it mentions those who, "Love God and keep His commandments" (Ex. 20:6, Deut. 5:10, Deut. 7:9, Deut. 11:1, Deut. 11:22, Deut. 19:9, Deut. 30:16, Josh. 22:5, Dan. 9:4, etc.). John was simply quoting the Old Testament when he said, "For this is the love (agapē) of God, that we keep his commandments" (1 John 3:4). To love God is to keep His commandments.

If loving God means keeping His commandments, the logical next question is, how does God love us? The Scripture is not silent on this matter either. In Prov. 3:12, the author states, "For whom YHVH loves he corrects; even as a father the son in whom he delights." This is repeated in Rev. 3:19 and Heb. 12:6-9. God will discipline all His children when they do wrong (sin). Though God disciplines His children, He also blesses them as well. Moses said,

> And [God] will love thee, and bless thee, and multiply thee: he will also bless the fruit of your womb, and the fruit of your land, your corn, and your wine, and your oil, the increase of your kind, and the flocks of your sheep, in the land which he swore unto your fathers to give you (Deut. 7:13).

God will bless His children when they do good and discipline His children when they do wrong (sin). These blessings and disciplines (or curses) are from the Mosaic covenant. In Leviticus 26 and Deuteronomy 28, God tells us that if we love Him (keep His commandments) He will bless us (Lev. 26:3-12, Deut. 28:1-14), but if we do not love Him (break His commandments) then He will curse us (Lev. 26:13-40, Deut. 28:15-45). This is what love is, the keeping of a contract.

The concept of love as the keeping of a contract may seem odd. Keep in mind, though, that the word contract is new and nowhere found in the Scripture. The word used for contract in the Scripture is covenant, which is found frequently in the Scripture. God offered this covenant/contract on Mount Sinai thousands of years ago. The terms of this contract are found in Exodus 19-24. The Israelites agreed to this contract by saying, "All that YHVH has said will we do, and be obedient" (Ex. 24:7). The parties to this contract are God and the Israelites (or anyone/nation who practices God's law). Each party has a duty under this contract which is explained in the Scripture. Man's duty is to "walk in [His] statutes, and keep [His] commandments, and do them" (Lev. 26:3, Deut.28:1). Solomon put it this way, "Let us hear the conclusion of the whole matter: Fear God, and keep his commandments: for this is the whole duty of man" (Eccl.

12:13). Man's duty under this contract is to obey God and keep His commandments. This is clear, but what is often forgotten is that God has a duty as well.

God's duty under this same contract is listed in Exodus 23, Leviticus 26, and Deuteronomy 28. God gives blessings and curses based on this law. If believers obey God and keep His commandments, God will bless His people (Lev. 26:3-12, Deut. 28:1-14). If believers do not obey God and keep His commandments, He will give curses (discipline) to His people (Lev. 26:13-40, Deut. 28:15-45). This is a duty that God is required to perform under this contract. This is why Moses described God as, "The faithful God, which keeps covenant and mercy with them that love him and keep his commandments to a thousand generations" (Deut. 7:9). Man's job, or consideration, is to keep His commandments and God's job, or consideration, is to provide blessings and curses based on man's performance. This is the contract of love. God loves us by keeping His end of the contract, and man loves Him by keeping their end of the contract. This is why the Messiah summed up the law and the prophets with two commandments, to love God and love your neighbor (Matt. 22:37-40). Every commandment in the Scripture fits under these two commands.

The problem man has is they are not able to keep up their end of this contract. They can try and try, but they will always fail. The Scripture is clear on this. The Apostle Paul said that, "All have sinned, and come short of the glory of God" (Rom. 3:23). This is why God sent His Holy Spirit. The Holy Spirit was sent to "reprove the world of sin, and of righteousness" (John 16:8). The Holy Spirit is a "comforter" to "abide with [us] forever" (John 14:16). The Greek word for comforter is παράκλητος (paraklētos) which literally means "called to one's side, called to one's aid."[72] This word is the word used for an advocate who stands beside a defendant to act as their lawyer in court. The Holy Spirit comes to one's side, so they can "walk in the Spirit", and so they do not "fulfil the lust of the flesh" (Gal. 5:16, Gal. 5:25). The only way man can love God and keep His commandments is to walk in His Spirit. Remember, Ezekiel 37:26 tells us that the Spirit was given that man might "walk in [His] statutes, and ... shall keep [His] judgments, and do them" (Eze. 36:27). The purpose of the Holy Spirit is to "reprove the world of sin" and "put [God's] law in [men's] hearts" (Jer. 31:33). The end result is man will "walk in the spirit" to aid them to "walk in [His] statutes ... and keep [His] judgments, and do them." Not only does God keep His end of this contract, but He also helps man keep their end. God has come along side man to help them love Him and practice His law. This is one of the Holy Spirit's jobs, to strengthen man's faith (1 Cor. 12:9, 2 Cor. 4:13). This faith helps man to keep God's commandments. The question that needs to be asked is, what is biblical faith?

What is Biblical Faith?

Faith is the answer to keeping God's commandments. Faith is the Greek word πίστις (pistis). This word has a different meaning than many people think. Faith means

---

[72] Thayer, Joseph H., "Comforter - παράκλητος - paraklētos." *Thayer's Greek-English Lexicon of the New Testament*, pg. 483, G3875.

"persuasion, that is, credence; moral conviction."[73] Those that have biblical faith have a strong moral conviction to be faithful in keeping God's commandments. This is the difference between the Old and New Covenants. When speaking of the Old Covenant the writer of Hebrews said, "For unto us was the gospel preached, as well as unto them: but the word preached did not profit them, **not being mixed with faith** in them that heard it" (Heb. 4:2). The Old Covenant failed because they did not mix it with faith. Repeatedly, God pleaded with Israel to believe in Him (Ex. 4:5, Ex. 19:9, Num. 14:11, Deut. 1:32, 2 Kings 17:14, 2 Chron. 20:20). Those in the Old Covenant needed to start with faith. After all, faith "establish[es] the law" (Rom. 3:31). Israel needed to first have a moral conviction and a strong fortitude to keep God's commandments. This moral conviction (faith) is easier under the New Covenant because we have seen God's promise. The writer of Hebrews listed several faithful believers in the Old Covenant in chapter eleven. At the end of the chapter he said, "And these all, having obtained a good report through faith, received not the promise" (Heb. 11:39-40). Those before the Messiah did not receive, or understand, the promise of faith. They did not understand the death, burial, and resurrection of the Messiah for the forgiveness of sins, yet they still had faith that God would forgive their sin.

This is how love and faith go hand in hand. The modern definition of love is so different than God's definition of love. Love is not a feeling that someone

---

[73] Strong, James, "Faith - πίστις - pistis." *A Concise Dictionary of the Words in the Greek Bible*, pg. 56, G4102.

places on something, but an action someone does as a result of something. That's what faith is for. Faith is having the moral conviction to love God and obey His commandments. Faith is having the moral conviction to love (agapē). While keeping God's commandments (love) is the duty of man, faith is the fuel to be successful. Just as a good father disciplines his children when they do wrong and blesses them when they do right, so God disciplines man when they sin and blesses them when they do right. This is what God calls love. Man can't just say they love God, they must show it also. As the modern saying goes, actions speak louder than words. God knows man loves Him by the actions of keeping His commandments. This is why understanding what covenant means is so important. Covenant brings faith and love into one.

What is a Covenant?

To better understand love and faith, it is needed to define the word covenant and identify the meaning of three main covenants God has with man. The Hebrew word for covenant is בְּרִית (berîyth) which means "covenant, alliance, pledge."[74] This is the scriptural word for contract. According to the Cornell Law School Wex Legal Dictionary,

> A covenant is a formal agreement or promise, usually included in a contract or deed, to do or not do a particular act. Covenants are particularly

---

[74] F. Brown, S. Driver, and C. Briggs, "Covenant – בְּרִית - berîyth." *The Brown-Driver-Briggs Hebrew and English Lexicon*, pg. 136, H1285.

relevant in the fields of contract law and property law. An example of a contractual covenant is a non-compete agreement. Examples of common covenants in property law include agreements not to build a fence or agreements to maintain a shared driveway. **Covenants in contract law are governed by standard contract rules and exclusively apply to the parties of the contract.**[75]

A covenant is a contract. According to Sir William Blackstone and his *Commentaries on the Laws of England*, "A contract, which usually conveys an interest merely in action, is thus defined; - an agreement, upon sufficient consideration, to do or not to do a particular thing."[76] A contract is making an agreement with another party to do, or not do, something. The modern term for covenant is contract. They are governed by the same rules and have the same expectations. When dealing with the covenants in the Scripture it is important to apply the legal rules for contract law.

According to *John Bouvier's Law Dictionary*, there are four elements to all contracts. First, there is always an offer. Second, this offer must be accepted. Third, the contract must contain a time limit and fourth there is always consideration. These four elements are in every contract. An offer in contracts, "is a proposition to do a thing. An offer ought to contain a right, if accepted, of compelling the fulfilment of the contract, and this right

---

[75] Wex Definitions Team, Wex Legal Information Institute, Cornell Law School, "Covenant." July of 2022, obtained June, 11, 2024, https://www.law.cornell.edu/wex/covenant
[76] Blackstone, Sir William, Knight, *Commentaries on the Laws of England*, (The Lawbook Exchange, LTD. Clark, New Jersey, 2011), pg. 897)

when not expressed, is always implied."[77] An offer must be made to initiate a contract and the offer always initiates a right to something. This contract is not valid until the offer is accepted. An acceptance in contracts is "an agreement to receive something which has been offered."[78] This is the act which authorizes the contract and establishes the rights to be received. The obligation of the contract is called consideration. Consideration in contracts "is the compensation which is paid, or inconvenience suffered by the party from which it flows."[79] The consideration contains each party's duty to the contract. This is the right, expressed or implied, from the offer and acceptance. When the contract is accepted one or both parties have a right to the consideration of the contract. Finally, there must be a time limit. Time in contracts is "the measure of duration. . . . Time is frequently of the essence of contracts and crimes, and sometimes it is altogether immaterial."[80] Without a time limit it is hard to enforce the contract. For example, if a contract was written to pay a sum of money by the end of the year, then at the end of the year the contract can be enforced. However, if a contract was written to pay a sum of money whenever someone is able, then the contract can only be enforced when one party can make the payment. Since there is no clear time limit, the contract

---

[77] Bouvier, John, "Law." *A Law Dictionary Adapted to the Constitution and Laws of the United States of America*, Vol. II, pg. 203.

[78] Bouvier, John, "Law." *A Law Dictionary Adapted to the Constitution and Laws of the United States of America*, Vol. I, pg. 34.

[79] Bouvier, John, "Law." *A Law Dictionary Adapted to the Constitution and Laws of the United States of America*, Vol. I, pg. 215.

[80] Bouvier, John, "Law." *A Law Dictionary Adapted to the Constitution and Laws of the United States of America*, Vol. II, pg. 439.

can feasibly go on forever without payment. This in effect can void the contract because the time limit is too vague and ambiguous. An example of a modern contract might be to build a pool in a backyard. A contractor might offer to do the job for $50,000. The homeowner can accept this contract or make a counter offer. Once there is a meeting of the minds, the offer is accepted. The contract might say the pool will be finished by a specific date or in a number of days, weeks, or months. The consideration of this contract is $50,000 to the contractor and a pool to the homeowner. See Table 5.

Four Elements to Contracts	
1. Offer	• Build a pool for $50,000
2. Acceptance	• Agree to the offer (might have counter offer first)
3. Time Limit	• By May 1, 2024
4. Consideration	• $50,000 to contractor ○ $50,000 to contractor ○ Pool to homeowner

Table 5

These are the four essential elements of all contracts from *Bouvier's Law Dictionary*. The point to all this is that these same four elements are part of the scriptural covenants as well. This will become clear as we look into the three main covenants of the Scripture. However, there are two more aspects of contracts to consider. There is always more than one party to every contract. These contracts can be either bilateral or unilateral. According to Henry Campbell Black and his law dictionary,

> A unilateral contract is one in which one party makes an express engagement or undertakes a performance, without receiving in return any express engagement or promise of performance from the other. Bilateral contracts are those by which the parties expressly enter into mutual engagements, such as sale or hire.[81]

The difference between a unilateral contract and a bilateral contract is the consideration. In a unilateral contract only one party has consideration. In a bilateral contract both parties have consideration. These definitions are very important to understand the covenants in the Scripture. When using these principles in studying the covenants within the Scripture things become very clear. With these definitions in mind the next chapter will take a look at the major Covenants found in the Scripture.

---

[81] Black, Henry Campbell, "Contracts – Unilateral and Bilateral." *Black's Law Dictionary*, Fifth Edition, pg. 294.

Chapter Seven

The Covenants of God

There are many covenants in the Scripture. God made a covenant with Adam to give him dominion over the earth. Then he lost that dominion, and God gave a curse on man and the earth. God made a covenant with Noah to not destroy the earth with a flood again. God made a covenant of promise to Abraham to provide the promised Messiah.   This is often just called The Promise, or the Abrahamic Covenant. God made a covenant with Moses and the Israelites. This is commonly called the Old Covenant, or Mosaic Covenant. God made a covenant with David that the Messiah would come from him and rule and reign on his throne. Finally, God made a covenant through the Messiah called the New Covenant. This covenant was for the forgiveness of sins.

Covenants in the Bible	
1.	Adamic Covenant	Curse of sin
2.	Noahic Covenant	No more flood
3.	*Abrahamic Covenant*	Promised Messiah
4.	*Old Covenant*	Law with blessings/curses
5.	Palestinian Covenant	Land to Israel
6.	Davidic Covenant	Messiah from line of David
7.	*New Covenant*	Forgiveness of sins

Table 6

Each of these covenants is significant in its own rights, but the focus of this chapter is only on three of these covenants. This chapter is going to discuss the significance of the Abrahamic Covenant, the Old Covenant, and the New Covenant and how these three covenants fit together.

The Abrahamic Covenant:

The Abrahamic Covenant is also known as the Covenant of Promise. Hebrews 11:39-40 says, "And these all, having obtained a good report through faith, **received not the promise**: God having provided some better thing for us, that they without us should not be made perfect." This contract is unilateral and contains all four elements from *Bouvier's Law Dictionary*. The promise to Abraham was for his seed. Paul said, "Now to Abraham and his seed were the promises made. He says not, and to seeds, as of many; but as of one, and to your seed, which is Christ" (Gal 3:16). The seed of Abraham is the Messiah and His atoning death, burial, and resurrection. The Messiah is the promise. This covenant is a unilateral contract between God and Abraham. We know this because this covenant was ratified with a burnt offering. Abraham asked God, "whereby shall I know that I shall inherit it?" (Gen. 15:8). God told Abraham,

> Take me a heifer of three years old, and a she goat of three years old, and a ram of three years old, and a turtledove, and a young pigeon. And he took unto him all these, and divided them in the midst, and laid each piece one against another: but the birds divided he not. (Gen. 15:9-10)

Then, God ratified the covenant with a burning lamp that passed between the pieces as recorded in Genesis 15.

> And it came to pass, that, when the sun went down, and it was dark, behold a smoking furnace, **and a burning lamp that passed between those pieces**. In the same day YHVH made a covenant with Abram, saying, unto your seed have I given this land, from the river of Egypt unto the great river, the river Euphrates. (Gen. 15:17-18)

God passed between the pieces of the burnt offerings to ratify the covenant. We know this was a method to ratify covenants from the book of Jeremiah. God told Jeremiah, "And I will give the men that have transgressed my covenant, which have not performed **the words of the covenant which they had made before me, when they cut the calf in two, and passed between the parts thereof**" (Jer. 34:18). Theologian John Gill put it this way,

> [This] was a rite or custom used in making and confirming covenants; a calf, or some other creature, were cut in pieces, and the parts laid in order, and the covenantees passed between these parts; signifying thereby, that if they did not fulfil

the engagements they entered into, they imprecated to be cut to pieces as that creature was.[82]

A burning lamp passes between the pieces. Gerard Hoet, 1728.

The interesting thing is that God is the only one who passed between the pieces. This is why it is a unilateral

---

[82] Gill, John, *John Gill's Exposition of the Bible*, Jeremiah 34:18, Obtained June 6, 2024, https://sacred-texts.com/bib/cmt/gill/jer034.htm.

contract. If this were a bilateral covenant, then both parties would have passed between the pieces. This covenant is certain to be fulfilled because God is the only party of this covenant that has any duties, and God is known as "the faithful God, which keeps covenant and mercy with them that love him and keep his commandments to a thousand generations" (Deut. 7:9). That is the Abrahamic Covenant. It is the covenant of the promised Messiah for the forgiveness of sins. It is the covenant of faith, which is why Paul said, "Even as **Abraham believed God**, and it was accounted to him for righteousness. Know you therefore that **they which are of faith**, the same are the children of Abraham" (Gal. 3:6-7, Gen. 15:6). Paul even clarified more when saying, "Now to Abraham and his seed were the promises made. He says not, and to seeds, as of many; but as of one, and to your seed, which is Christ" (Gal 3:16). The Abrahamic Covenant is the covenant of faith in the Messiah of Israel.

Four Elements of the Covenant of Promise	
1. Offer	• Promised Messiah from Abraham's seed (Gen. 12-17)
2. Acceptance	• Abraham believed God (Gen. 15:6)
3. Time	• Forever (Gen. 13:5)
4. Consideration	• Provide salvation through Messiah ○ Unilateral Contract: God has consideration, but not man.

Table 8

The Old Covenant:

The Old Covenant, also known as the Mosaic Covenant, is a bilateral contract. The contract has two parties, God and the children of Israel. Both of these parties have duties and obligations within this contract. This contract is recorded in the book of Exodus. God said to Moses,

> Thus shall you say to the house of Jacob, and tell the children of Israel; you have seen what I did unto the Egyptians, and how I bare you on eagles' wings, and brought you unto myself. **Now therefore, if you will obey my voice indeed, and keep my covenant, then you shall be a peculiar treasure unto me above all people**: for all the earth is mine: And you shall be unto me a kingdom of priests, and a holy nation. These are the words which you shall speak unto the children of Israel. (Ex. 19:3-6)

This is the offer that God gave to Moses and the children of Israel. This is the very first step to initiate a contract. The next two verses contain the acceptance.

> And Moses came and called for the elders of the people, and laid before their faces all these words which YHVH commanded him. And all the people answered together, and said, **all that YHVH hath spoken we will do**. And Moses returned the words of the people unto YHVH. (Ex. 19:7-8)

This offer with an acceptance identifies the two parties to the contract. The Old Covenant is between God and the children of Israel. It is important to note that although this covenant is with the children of Israel, foreigners were to keep it as well. At the instruction of the Passover, God said, "One law shall be to him that is homeborn, and unto the stranger that sojourns among you" (Ex. 12:49). This is confirmed again in the book of Leviticus when God said, "But the stranger that dwells with you shall be unto you as one born among you, and you shall love him as yourself; for you were strangers in the land of Egypt: I am YHVH your God" (Lev. 19:34). There are numerous other verses which state this as well (Ex. 12: 19, 43, 48-49, 22:21, 23;9, 23:12, 29:33, 30:33, Lev. 16:29, 17:12, 15, 18:26, 19:10, 24:16, 22, 25:6, 25:35, 25:47, Num. 9:14, 15:14-16, 26-30, 19:10, 35:15, Deut. 5:14, 10:18-19, 14:29, 16:11-14, 24:17-19, 24:20-21, 26:11-13, 27:19, 28:43, 29:11, 22, 31:12). The point is that this covenant was made with God and the children of Israel. The stranger that lived with Israel was also part of this covenant.

God then lists the terms of the covenant by coming down to Mount Sinai and giving Moses His Law in the next four chapters. These chapters contain the consideration of the contract. Man's duty is to obey the Law of God (Ex. 20:1-23:33). God said to Moses, "And shewing mercy unto thousands of them that love me, and **keep my commandments**" (Ex. 20:6). God's duty is to give blessings and curses based upon our obedience to that law (Ex. 23:25-31, Lev. 26, Deut. 28). In fact, God spends two entire chapters, Leviticus 26 and Deuteronomy 28, explaining His duties to this contract. The time limit is clearly forever for God said so numerous times (Ex. 12:14, Ex. 12:17, Ex. 12:24, Ex. 17:21, Ex. 28:43, Ex. 29:28, Ex. 30:21, Ex. 31:17, Ex. 32:13, Lev. 6:18, Lev. 6:22, Lev. 7:34, Lev. 7:36, Lev. 10:9, Lev. 10:15, Lev. 16:29, Lev. 16:31, Lev. 23:14, Lev. 23:21, Lev. 23:41, Lev. 24:3, Lev. 25:23, Lev. 25:46, Num.

10:8, Num. 15:15, Num. 18:8, Num. 18:11, Num. 18:19, Num. 18:23, Num. 19:10, Deut. 4:40, Deut. 18:5, Deut. 19:9, Deut. 23:3, Deut. 28:46). This covenant was then confirmed when Moses,

> wrote all the words of YHVH, and rose up early in the morning, and built an altar under the hill, and twelve pillars, according to the twelve tribes of Israel. And he sent young men of the children of Israel, which offered **burnt offerings**, and sacrificed peace offerings of oxen unto YHVH. And Moses took half of the blood, and put it in basins; and half of the blood he sprinkled on the altar. And he took the book of the covenant, and read in the audience of the people: and they said, **all that YHVH has said will we do, and be obedient.** And Moses took the blood, and **sprinkled it on the people**, and said, Behold the blood of the covenant, which YHVH has made with you concerning all these words. And Moses took the blood, and sprinkled it on the people, and said, Behold the blood of the covenant, which YHVH has made with you concerning all these words. (Ex. 24:4-8).

This contract was now ratified with a burnt offering (Ex. 24:5). This is a bilateral contract because there are two parties involved, the children of Israel and YHVH. The offer was given and accepted by Israel when they said, "will we do, and be obedient." This is signified by the sprinkling of blood on the people from the burnt offering. The consideration was clear and a time limit was stated. The only thing that can end this contract is a breach of the contract by one or both parties.

Four Elements of the Old Covenant	
1. Offer	• YHVH will be their God (Ex. 19:3-6)
2. Acceptance	• "all that YHVH hath spoken we will do" (Ex. 19:7-8)
3. Time	• "believe you forever" (Ex. 19:9)

4. Consideration	• Obedience to God's law (Lev. 26 & Deut. 28)
	   ○ Man – keep commandments
	   ○ God – keep commandments and give blessings/curses.

Table 9

The New Covenant:

The New Covenant is not any different than the Old Covenant. This might seem like a strange statement, but consider the following. The New Covenant is also a bilateral contract. The parties involved are God and the children of Israel. Here is what the prophet Jeremiah said.

> Behold, the days come, says YHVH, that **I will make a new covenant with the house of Israel, and with the house of Judah**: Not according to the covenant that I made with their fathers in the day that I took them by the hand to bring them out of the land of Egypt; which my covenant they broke, although I was a husband unto them, says YHVH: But this shall be the covenant that I will make with the **house of Israel**; After those days, says YHVH, **I will put my law in their inward parts, and write it in their hearts**; and will be their God, and they shall be my people. (Jer. 31:31-33)

From this statement a couple of significant aspects of the New Covenant can be learned. First, the parties to the contract are God and the children of Israel. Second, the New Covenant contains the Law of God. The Law of God is the consideration of the New Covenant. The offer was

The Last Supper with bread and wine, James Tissot, 1886-1894.

made at the last supper when the Messiah said, "And he took the cup, and gave thanks, and gave it to them, saying, drink you all of it; for **this is my blood of the new testament [covenant]**, which is shed for many for the remission of sins" (Matt. 26:27-28). Just as the Old Covenant was ratified with the blood of a burnt offering sprinkled on the people (Ex. 24:5, 8), the New Covenant was ratified with the Messiah's blood (Matt. 26:27-28). The offer was given and the apostles accepted the offer when they drank of the wine, which represents the Messiah's blood. The New Covenant still contains the Law of God. Jeremiah said, "I will put my law in their inward parts, and write it in their hearts" (Jer. 31:33). Under the New Covenant our duty is to obey the commandments, statutes, and judgments of God (Ex. 24:7). In fact, the Messiah taught the same thing when He said,

> Think not that I am come to destroy the law, or the prophets: I am not come to destroy, but to fulfil. **For verily I say unto you, till heaven and earth pass, one jot or one tittle shall in no wise pass from the law, till all be fulfilled**. Whosoever therefore shall break one of these least commandments, and shall teach men so, he shall be called the least in the kingdom of heaven: but whosoever shall do and teach them, the same shall be called great in the kingdom of heaven. (Matt. 5:17-19)

The Messiah endorsed the practice of God's law emphatically. He even endorsed the "least commandments" as well. Many times, the Messiah said, "If you love me, keep my commandments" (John 14:15). It has already been shown that throughout the New Testament believers are told to keep God's commandments numerous times (Matt. 19:17, John 15:10, 1 John 2:3, 1 John 3:22, 1 John 5:2-3, Rev. 12:17, Rev. 14:12). Man's duty is the same as the Old Covenant, to keep the Law of God. God's duty is the same as the Old Covenant as well. God keeps His own commandments, and He provides blessings and curses based on man's obedience to those commandments. The New Testament even quotes the Old Testament saying,

> And you have forgotten the exhortation which speaks unto you as unto children, My son, despise not **the chastening of the Lord**, nor faint when you are rebuked of him: **For whom the Lord loves he chastens, and scourges every son whom he receives**. If you endure chastening, God deals with you as with sons; for what son is he whom the father chastens not? But if you be without

> chastisement, whereof all are partakers, then are you bastards, and not sons. Furthermore, we have had fathers of our flesh which corrected us, and we gave them reverence: shall we not much rather be in subjection unto the Father of spirits, and live? (Heb. 12:5-9)

God disciplines those in the New Covenant just like He did with those of the Old Covenant. The terms of the New Covenant are the same as the terms of the Old Covenant. There is no difference except with one qualification.

The Old Covenant failed for one reason, a lack of faith. Here are some points to consider. First, remember that those in the Old Testament were saved the same way as the New Testament. Paul said "Abraham believed God, and it was accounted to him for righteousness" (Gal. 3:6). Paul was quoting Gen. 15:6 which says, "And he believed in YHVH; and he counted it to him for righteousness." Abraham's salvation was based upon faith (belief). Second, the gospel was preached to those in the Old Covenant. Hebrews 4:2 says, "For unto us was the gospel preached, **as well as unto them**: but the word preached did not profit them, **not being mixed with faith** in them that heard it." The Apostle Paul agrees when he said, "And the Scripture, foreseeing that God would justify the heathen through faith, preached before the gospel unto Abraham, saying, In you shall all nations be blessed" (Gal. 3:8). The gospel in the Old Testament is found in Genesis 12:3 and Genesis 18:18. Genesis 12:3 says, "And I will bless them that bless you, and curse him that curses you: and in you shall all families of the earth be blessed." This is repeated again in Genesis 18:18 which says, "Seeing that Abraham shall surely become a great and mighty nation, and all the nations of the earth shall be blessed in him?" This is the gospel message; that the Messiah would die, get buried, and rise again to bless all the nations of the world so they can come back into covenant with God.

The Abrahamic Covenant was a unilateral covenant where God promised that through Abraham's seed the Messiah would come and bless all nations of the earth with his atoning sacrifice. Paul said, "Now to Abraham and his seed were the promises made. He said not, and to seeds, as of many; but as of one, and to your seed, which is Messiah" (Gal. 3:16). The word for seed is singular and represents one person, the Messiah. The gospel preached unto Abraham was the Covenant of Promise to bless all nations with the coming Messiah.   This promise was that The Old Covenant only failed because it was "not being mixed with faith in them that heard it" (Heb. 4:2). The reason it failed was not because the covenant was bad, but because the people broke the covenant. The writer to Hebrews said,

> For if that first covenant had been faultless, then should no place have been sought for the second. **For finding fault with them**, he says, Behold, the days come, says YHVH, when I will make a new covenant with the house of Israel and with the house of Judah. (Heb. 8:8-9)

The fault was not with God or with the covenant. The fault was with the people of Israel. The people of Israel were in breach of contract. This is why God divorced Israel in the book of Jeremiah. The prophet Jeremiah said,

> And I said after she had done all these things, Turn you unto me. But she returned not. And her

> treacherous sister Judah saw it. And I saw, when for all the causes whereby **backsliding Israel committed adultery I had put her away, and given her a bill of divorce**; yet her treacherous sister Judah feared not, but went and played the harlot also. And it came to pass through the lightness of her whoredom, that she defiled the land, and committed adultery with stones and with stocks. And yet for all this her treacherous sister Judah has not turned unto me with her whole heart, but feignedly, says YHVH. (Jer. 3:7-10)

God divorced Israel because He "found some uncleanness in her" (Deut. 24:1). This is the law for divorce in the Old Testament. To get a divorce you must find "some uncleanness," or breach of contract, with the other party. God followed His own law when divorcing Israel. This severed the Old Covenant with Israel, but what about Judah? When God sent the Messiah to the house of Judah then the Old Covenant with Judah was also severed because of their rejection of him. There are two ways a covenant can end: termination (divorce) or death. The Messiah's death on the cross severed the contract with Judah. At this point, the Old Covenant is over which makes way for a New Covenant. The question is still at hand, what is the difference between the Old and New Covenants? Here is the simple answer. The difference between the Old and New Covenants is the Abrahamic Covenant.

Four Elements of the New Covenant	
1. Offer	• Blood of the covenant (Matt. 26:27-28)
2. Acceptance	• Drank the wine at the Last Supper (Mark 14:23)
3. Time	• Forever (Heb. 13:20)

4. Consideration	• Obedience to God's law (1 John 2:3, 5:2-3 & Heb. 12:6)
	    ○ Man – keep commandments
	    ○ God – keep commandments by giving blessings/curses.

Table 10

How the Covenants Fit Together:

The difference that makes the New Covenant better than the Old Covenant is the Abrahamic Covenant. The New Covenant is simply the Old Covenant and the Abrahamic Covenant together. The Apostle Paul said, "And this I say, that the covenant, that was confirmed before of God in Christ, the law, which was four hundred and thirty years after, **cannot disannul, that it should make the promise of none effect**" (Gal. 3:17). The Old Covenant was four hundred years later than the Abrahamic Covenant. The Old Covenant was supposed to start with the Abrahamic Covenant. The Old Covenant was supposed to start with faith. The Covenant of Promise was given to Abraham, but Abraham did not know the details. He did not receive the promise (Heb. 11:39-40), but he did believe in God's promise. The New Covenant is that same promise. In the New Covenant the promised Messiah is seen in more detail. It is now known how he will bring nations back to God. This is the only difference, but it is big. Abraham believed, but he did not know the details of how God was going to fulfill His promise. Today in the New Covenant, men can still believe, but now they know how God fulfilled His promise. When the Law was given on Mount Sinai, they were supposed to mix it with faith. Over and over again God said to "believe" Him (Ex. 4:5-9, Ex. 4:31, Ex. 19:9, Num. 12:7, Num. 14:11, Num. 20:12, Deut. 1:32, Deut. 9:23, etc.). They were supposed to believe in God like Abraham did (mix it with faith Heb. 4:2), but they did not. When someone really believes God, His Law will be written on their heart (Jer. 31:31). This is much easier today because there is more knowledge of the promised Messiah than Abraham had. Today, the gospel preached to Abraham is understood much more than in Abraham's day. This understanding is of the death, burial, and resurrection of the Messiah.

Remember the definition of faith. Faith (pistis - G4102) is "persuasion, that is, credence; moral conviction."[83] Believers should be persuaded and have a strong moral conviction to follow the Messiah. This is such a strong conviction that believers can't help but follow the Messiah. Believers have now seen what God has done for them in the death, burial, and resurrection of the Messiah, so that they should be morally persuaded to do His will, and God's will is His Law. Man has a duty to keep God's Commandments. They are to, "Fear God, and keep his commandments: for this is the whole duty of man" (Eccl.

---

[83] Strong, James, "Faith - pistis." *A Concise Dictionary of the Words in the Greek Bible*, pg. 58, G4102.

12:13). This is God writing His Law on their hearts. When man has this kind of faith they become faithful and keep His commandments. When man sees the promised Messiah and what God has given up to forgive their sins, they are given a heart to keep God's commandments (law written on their hearts – Jer. 31:33). It is easier now in the New Covenant because the promise of God is known. Abraham believed even though he did not see God's promise. That is why he is the father of faith. He believed without seeing.

There is very little difference between the Old and New Covenants. The Old Covenant was supposed to be mixed with faith, which is the Covenant of Promise. The New Covenant is the Promise (faith) and God's law written on our hearts. The only difference is that today man has been privileged to see God's promised Messiah in the New Covenant. Paul said,

> Now to Abraham and his seed were the promises made. He says not, and to seeds, as of many; but as of one, and to your seed, which is Christ. And this I say, that the covenant, that was confirmed before of God in Christ, the law, which was four hundred and thirty years after, **cannot disannul**, that it should make the promise of none effect. (Gal 3:16-17)

Those of the Old Covenant were not supposed to "disannul" the Covenant of Promise (faith). They were always supposed to believe in God, even though they did not know the details of God's promise to Abraham. This is why the Messiah said, "Your father Abraham rejoiced to see my day: and he saw it, and was glad" (John 8:58).

Abraham did not physically see the Messiah, but he did see him by faith. The New Covenant is better because man has seen God's plan unfolded through the Messiah. Abraham knew God was going to forgive his sins, but he did not know how. Today God's plan through the Messiah is known. This makes it easier to have faith because God's plan is clear. The New Covenant is what the Old Covenant was supposed to be. The New Covenant is the Old Covenant mixed with the Abrahamic Covenant. The New Covenant is the Old Covenant mixed with faith.

Chapter Eight

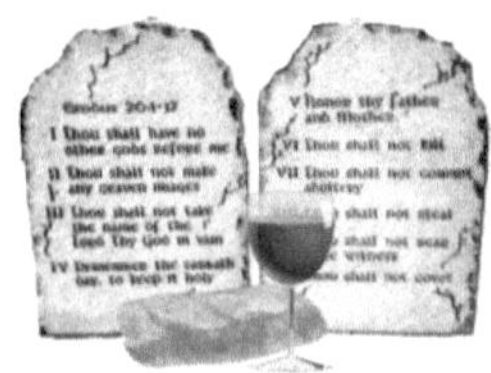

God is Building Nations, Not Religions

The Old Covenant and the New Covenant are national covenants. They are covenants God made "with the house of Israel, and with the house of Judah" (Jer. 31:31). God is dealing with nations, not religions. After the flood of Noah, God spoke to a man named Abram. God told Abram, "Get ye out of your country, and from your kindred, and from your father's house, unto a land that I will shew you: And **I will make of you a great nation**, and I will bless you, and make your name great; and you shall be a blessing:" (Gen. 12:1-2). God called

Map of the Holy Land, Emanuel

Abram out of his country to start a new nation. In fact, God told Abram he would "be a father of many nations" (Gen. 17:4). This is what the name Abraham means. Abram is the Hebrew word אַבְרָם ('abrâm) which means "exalted father."[84] The Hebrew word for Abraham is אַבְרָהָם ('abrâhâm) and means "father of a multitude" or "chief of multitude."[85] This is why God said to Abram, "Neither shall your name any more be called Abram, but your name shall be Abraham; **for a father of many nations have I made you**" (Gen. 17:5). God's plan was to make many nations from the faith of one man. God is building nations and not religions. This is the point to this entire book series. God started out building nations, and He is still building nations today.

The Hebrew word for "nations" is גּוֹי (gôy), which means, "nation, people, usually of non-Hebrew people."[86] This word represents a group of people who live together under a national law. We know this because two verses later God said to Abraham, "I will make you exceedingly fruitful, and I will make nations of you, and **kings shall come out of you**" (Gen. 17:6). God is building nations out of a man named Abraham. These nations started with one family and have grown from there. These nations will have kings and governments. Then, "God said unto Abraham, you shall keep my covenant therefore, you, and your seed after you in their generations" (Gen. 17:9). These nations

---

[84] F. Brown, S. Driver, and C. Briggs, "Abram – 'abrâm." *The Brown-Driver-Briggs Hebrew and English Lexicon*, pg. 8, H87.

[85] F. Brown, S. Driver, and C. Briggs, "Abram – 'abrâm." *The Brown-Driver-Briggs Hebrew and English Lexicon*, pg. 7, H85.

[86] F. Brown, S. Driver, and C. Briggs, "Nations – gôy." *The Brown-Driver-Briggs Hebrew and English Lexicon*, pg. 156, H1471.

will keep God's covenant with Abraham. These nations will have faith in the God of Abraham. These nations will keep God's commandments, statutes, and judgments in the faith of the Messiah of Israel.

Throughout the rest of Scripture is a history of the nation of Israel and their relationship with YHVH and the nations of the world. Although, most of this history deals with how God deals with Israel, there are times when God dealt with Gentile nations as well. Prior to Israel, God dealt with Sodom and Gomorrah (Gen. 13-14). He also dealt with Nineveh in the book of Jonah. God dealt with Babylon through King Nebuchadnezzar, and also with Medo-Persia, Greece, and Rome through Daniel's vision of the statue (Dan. 2). In fact, Psalms 117 is a call for Gentile nations to worship YHVH. Psalms 117:1-2 says, "O praise YHVH, all you nations: praise him, all you people. For his merciful kindness is great toward us: and the truth of YHVH endures forever. Praise you YHVH." Throughout the Scripture, God is dealing with both Israel and Gentile nations. All nations are required to keep God's commandments. At the second coming, the Messiah will judge the nations in their accordance in keeping His law.

> When the Son of man shall come in his glory, and all the holy angels with him, then shall he sit upon the throne of his glory: **And before him shall be gathered all nations**: and he shall separate them one from another, as a shepherd divides his sheep from the goats" (Matt. 25:31-32).

God is dealing both with nations and individuals. God will judge the nations through the Messiah for their obedience to His national law. God is also going to judge individuals and their works within their respective nation. This is why James said, "Faith without works is dead" (James 2:26). The works of the law validates faith. Even in the book of the Revelation, God is dealing with nations. "Who shall not fear you, O Lord, and glorify your name? for you only are holy: for all nations shall come and worship before you; for your judgments are made manifest (Rev. 15:4)." This judgment will be at the second coming. After that will be a thousand years of the kingdom of God ruled by the Messiah. Again, from beginning to end, God is building nations.

The History of Nations:

Throughout the Scripture God gives us the history of the nations. Specifically, God gives us the history of the nation of Israel. This history of Israel serves as an example for other nations to follow. When God's law was given to Moses he warned Israel,

> Behold, I have taught you statutes and judgments, even as YHVH my God commanded me, that you should do so in the land whither you go to possess it. **Keep therefore and do them; for this is your wisdom and your understanding in the sight of the nations**, which shall hear all these statutes, and say, surely this great nation is a wise and understanding people. For what nation is there so great, who has God so nigh unto them, as YHVH our God is in all things that we call upon him for? And what nation is there so great, that has statutes and judgments so righteous as all this law, which I set before you this day? (Deut. 4:5-8).

Israel was to be an example for other nations to follow. The Apostle Paul said the same thing.

> Behold, you are called a Jew, and rest in the law, and make your boast of God, and know his will, and approve the things that are more excellent, being instructed out of the law; and are confident that you yourself are a **guide of the blind**, **a light of them which are in darkness**, **an instructor of the foolish**, **a teacher of babes**, which has the form of knowledge and of the truth in the law" (Rom. 2:17-20).

Paul confirms that the Jews who were blessed with God's law should lead those who do not have God's law. This was the ultimate purpose of Israel. They were not to keep God to themselves. They were to share the light that God gave them to other nations. They were the example given for all nations to follow. Perhaps the best example of this is when the Queen of Sheba visited Solomon.

> And when the queen of Sheba heard of the fame of Solomon concerning the name of YHVH, she came to prove him with hard questions. And she came to Jerusalem with a very great train, with camels that bare spices, and very much gold, and precious stones: and when she was come to Solomon, she communed with him of all that was in her heart. And Solomon told her all her questions: there was not anything hid from the king, which he told her not. And when the queen of Sheba had seen all Solomon's wisdom, and the house that he had built, And the meat of his table, and the sitting of his servants, and the attendance of his ministers, and their apparel, and his cupbearers, and his ascent by which he went up

unto the house of YHVH; there was no more spirit in her. And she said to the king, **It was a true report that I heard in mine own land of your acts and of your wisdom.** Howbeit I believed not the words, until I came, and mine eyes had seen it: and, behold, the half was not told me: your wisdom and prosperity exceed the fame which I heard. Happy are your men, happy are these your servants, which stand continually before you, and that hear your wisdom. **Blessed be YHVH your God, which delighted in you, to set you on the throne of Israel: because YHVH loved Israel forever, therefore made he your king, to do judgment and justice.** And she gave the king a hundred and twenty talents of gold, and of spices very great store, and precious stones: there came no more such abundance of spices as these which the queen of Sheba gave to king Solomon. (1 Kings 10:1-10)

The Queen of Sheba heard of the fame and fortune of King Solomon and Israel. She had to see for herself, and she was amazed at the truth of what she had heard. This was the plan for Israel, to be an example nation to the rest

The Queen of Sheba visits Solomon. O. A. Stemler and Bess Bruce Cleaveland, 1929.

of the world. Unfortunately, Israel failed that mission, but today, nations can still learn from ancient Israel. The good things they did should be followed and the bad things they did should be avoided. The following is a short description of the history of Israel as an example nation for the world.

It is often said that the nation of Israel started out in slavery. The truth, however, is somewhat different. Israel did not start in slavery, but rather they started in bond servitude. The difference is significant. According to John Bouvier's, a slave is;

> A man who is by law deprived of his liberty for life, and becomes the property of another. A slave has no political rights, and generally has no civil rights. He can enter into no contract unless specially authorized by law; what he acquires generally, belongs to his master. The children of female slaves follow the condition of their mothers, and are themselves slaves."[87]

A slave does not have any rights and cannot own any property. When Moses spoke to Pharaoh to let the Hebrews go to the wilderness to serve God, he said, "We will go with our young and with our old, with our sons and with our daughters, **with our flocks and with our herds** will we go; for we must hold a feast unto YHVH" (Ex. 10:9). It is important to note that the Israelites had flocks and herds of animals. In fact, they had houses as well (Ex. 12:4). They had property and could not be categorized as slaves. Rather, the Israelites would have been categorized more like bondservants. A bondservant has many meanings in

---

[87] Bouvier, John, "Slave." *A Law Dictionary Adapted to the Constitution and Laws of the United States of America*, Vol. II, pg. 402.

the Scripture. The most prominent meaning is that of a slave. However, many times it refers to someone who has a higher status than a slave. The Hebrew word for slave/servant is עֶבֶד (`ebed), which means, "slave, servant, man-servant, subjects"[88] This word can have multiple meanings. In the case of the Israelites it means bondservant. This is clarified by the word used to describe the rulers in Egypt. When describing the Egyptian rulers, the Scripture uses the word "taskmasters" (Ex. 1:11). This is a combination of two words. The first word is שַׂר (śar) and means, "a head person (of any rank or class): - captain, chief, general, governor, ruler"[89] This word represents a ruler, or person in authority. The second word is מַס (mas) and means, "properly a burden (as causing to faint), that is, a tax in the form of forced labor: - discomfited, levy, task [-master], tribute (-tary)"[90] This word is almost always translated as tribute or tributaries. This word means they were taxed. The two words together means they had "rulers" who "taxed" them. This type of servitude was not entirely like slavery. Remember, many times the Israelites murmured in the wilderness and wanted to go back to Egypt (Num. 14:2). They were held under tribute in Egypt, but they had homes and property like herds and flocks (Ex. 10:8-9). They were not slaves as most think, but were subjects to another nation. This would not be much different than the American colonies being taxed by Britain. During the American Revolution, Britain enacted

---

[88] F. Brown, S. Driver, and C. Briggs, "Slave/servant – `ebed." *The Brown-Driver-Briggs Hebrew and English Lexicon*, pg. 713, H5650.

[89] Strong, James, "Taskmasters - śar." *A Concise Dictionary of the Words in the Hebrew Bible*, pg. 121, H6680.

[90] Strong, James, "Taskmasters - mas." *A Concise Dictionary of the Words in the Hebrew Bible*, pg. 68, H4522.

legislation over the American colonies. The Proclamation of 1763 forbade settlement. The Currency Act of 1764 regulated paper money. The Stamp Act of 1765 imposed a direct tax. Britain tried to hold the American Colonies under tribute as subjects. The American colonies had "taskmasters" and they wanted their freedom so the colonies chose to "exodus" from Britain and start their own nation. This is one example of the history of a nation and how they can learn from the nation of Israel.

The Israelites were not a free people so God "exodused" them from Egypt "with a mighty hand" (Deut. 6:21). God fought their battles for them with ten plagues. He turned water to blood, sent frogs, lice, flies, and caused the Egyptian animals to die. He then cursed the Egyptians with boils, hail, locusts, darkness, and finally the death of their firstborn. This is the mighty hand of God freeing His people. The same is true for America. In Brooklyn Heights, the American troops were outnumbered and in mortal danger. However, they were able to escape the British troops due to a heavy fog. In Dorchester Heights, bad weather prevented British troops from attacking. In the Battle of New Orleans, Andrew Jackson and his troops were outnumbered ten to one, yet they were still victorious. Stories like these are common when it comes to the American Revolution. President George Washington addressed this in his first inaugural address when he said,

> No people can be bound to acknowledge and adore the **Invisible Hand** which conducts the affairs of men more than the people of the United States. Every step by which they have advanced to the character of an independent nations seems

to have been distinguished by some token of **providential agency**. . . . We ought to be no less persuaded that the **propitious smiles of Heaven** can never be expected on a nation that disregards the **eternal rules of order and right** which Heaven itself has ordained."[91]

George Washington believed that America received God's providential protection because they followed God's "eternal rules of order," or in other words, God's law. Many do not realize that the Torah is the foundational law of the United States of America. Today, however, it is not called the Torah. It is simply called the Common Law, which will be discussed in more detail later in this chapter. Sadly, God's law has since been watered down in America, but it is this law that made America the best nation on the planet and it is the law that has sustained America for over two-hundred years. This law, God's law, is vitally important to maintain a strong nation. Remember, the rise and fall of every nation is based on whether they are obedient or disobedient to God's law.

The Time of the Judges:

After Israel wandered in the wilderness for forty years to remove a generation of murmuring people, they were given judges to rule the people (Judges 2:18). A judge is the Hebrew word שָׁפַט (shâphaṭ) which means, "to judge, that is, pronounce sentence (for or against); by implication

---

[91] Washington, George. "Washington's Inaugural Address", https://www.archives.gov/exhibits/american_originals/inaugtxt.html, April 30, 1789.

to vindicate or punish"[92] During this time the rulers of Israel were judges. God established a judicial system to govern the people. This time period is described throughout the book of Judges. This time of the judges is typically thought to be anarchy; however, there are many assumptions made that lead us to this false understanding. This might be surprising, but the book of Judges is not anarchy, but liberty.

The time of the judges was a very unique period in Israelite history. The Scripture teaches many things about Israel during this time. This time period is recorded in the book of Judges. There is a common phrase throughout this book. "In those days there was no king in Israel, but every man did that which was right in his own eyes" (Judges 17:6, 18:1, 19:1, 21:25). There are two things we can learn from this phrase. First, this was a time when there was no king in Israel, and second, the people did what they wanted to do. This phrase is usually understood as a very negative phrase; however, the Hebrew is neutral. This phrase is not stating a negative or positive. It is simply a phrase used to describe that period of time. There are two actual aspects of this phrase.

First, during the time of the judges Israel did not have a king; God was their king. Remember, the Israelites tried to place Gideon as their king, but Gideon refused and said, "I will not rule over you, neither shall my son rule over you: **YHVH shall rule over you**" (Judges 8:23). During the time of the judges, when there was no king over Israel, God was their King. This is confirmed later in the book of Samuel.

---

[92] Strong, James, "Judge - shâphaṭ." *A Concise Dictionary of the Words in the Hebrew Bible*, pg. 120, H8199.

When Israel tried to anoint a king, God was very disappointed. His response confirms that God rules when there is no king. "And YHVH said unto Samuel, hearken unto the voice of the people in all that they say unto you: for they have not rejected you, **but they have rejected me, that I should not reign over them**" (1 Sam. 8:7). When the people anointed a king, they removed God as their king.

Second, during the time of the judges the people did what was right in their own eyes. This, too, is a neutral phrase. This phrase is not implying a right or wrong doing, but is simply implying freedom. God's law is the "perfect law of liberty" (James 1:25). This is the freedom given under the Law of God. It is true that many people chose to do wrong, but God's judicial system dealt with each of these wrongs. God's law allows people the freedom to choose how to live their lives. This is God as the King of the nation. The nation had one law (God's law) that was never to change and a judicial system to construe that unchanging law and govern the people. This is a theocracy, not a monarchy, but especially not anarchy.

Rabbi Ken Spiro confirms this thought in his book, *Crash Course in Jewish History*. In Course fifteen titled, "The Time of the Judges", Spiro says,

> The Talmud calls the book of Judges, 'the Book of the Straight.' Why? Because the ultimate goal of every Jew is to use his free will to work out what is wrong and right, using the Torah as a guide. And this is what happens in the Time of Judges. In those days, there was no king in Israel, everyone did what was right in his eyes (Judges 21:25). You might think that this verse sounds like a description of anarchy. But there was no anarchy;

the vast majority of Jews were totally dedicated to Torah and were making decisions in the right way, and didn't need someone to tell them what to do. Indeed, that is the ideal situation. The tribes functioned as a loose confederation of states with strong central leadership arising only when the nation was threatened by an external enemy.[93]

Rabbi Ken Spiro points out some important points. First, this phrase is a neutral phrase. This is not a description of anarchy, but of freedom. The Israelites had the opportunity to choose between right and wrong. This is the "perfect law of liberty" that the Apostle James describes (James 1:25). God wants people to "work out what is wrong and right, using the Torah as a guide" as stated by Rabbi Ken Spiro. In fact, this sounds very familiar to what the Apostle Paul said. "Wherefore, my beloved, as you have always obeyed, not as in my presence only, but now much more in my absence, work out your own salvation with fear and trembling. For it is God which works in you both to will and to do of his good pleasure." (Phil. 2:12-13). This is a partnership between the believer and God. The believer is to work to become the man the Torah describes. James has a similar context when he said,

> But be you doers of the word, and not hearers only, deceiving your own selves. For if any be a hearer of the word, and not a doer, he is like unto a man beholding his natural face in a glass: For he beholds himself, and goes his way, and straightway forgets what manner of man he was. **But whoso looks into the perfect law of**

---

[93] Spiro, Rabbi Ken, *Crash Course in Jewish History*, Judaism 101, Aish.com. June 27th, 2020.

> **liberty**, and continues therein, he being not a forgetful hearer, but a doer of the work, this man shall be blessed in his deed" (James 1:22-25).

James is saying the same thing about God's law as Rabbi Spiro says. God's people are to "look into the perfect law of liberty" and judge themselves to make changes. This is freedom. This is liberty. This is God ruling His people through a priesthood and a temple.

This history of Israel is not much different than the history of America. Thomas Jefferson is often attributed with saying, "That government is best which governs the least, because its people discipline themselves." Thomas Jefferson may or may not have said this, but the idea was prevalent during his time. Henry David Thoreau did use a very similar phrase in his book *Civil Disobedience*. To start the book Thoreau wrote, "I heartily accept the motto, 'That government is best which governs least; and I should like to see it acted up to more rapidly and systematically."[94] When Judges uses the phrase, "In those days there was no king in Israel, but every man did that which was right in his own eyes" (Judges 17:6) it is speaking of the concept of limited government, not anarchy. The time of the Judges of ancient Israel is remarkably similar to colonial America. During this time "there was no President in America, everyone had the freedom to do their own will." This was limited government at its finest. This was the perfect law of liberty for the American people. As Rabbi Ken Spiro said, "The tribes functioned as a loose confederation of states with

---

[94] Thoreau, Henry David, *On the Duty of Civil Disobedience*, Salt Lake City, Utah, Libertas Institute, 1849, pg. 1.

strong central leadership arising only when the nation was threatened by an external enemy." This is a perfect description of the time of the judges and also a perfect description of colonial America. America also had a "loose confederation of states" that banded together when "threatened by an external enemy." The time of the judges for Israel was just before they anointed their first king. Colonial America is a similar time period for America and was also just before America inaugurated its first president.

A King Anointed:

The transition from judges to kings is found in the book of 1 Samuel. At the end of the time of the judges Israel was ruled by one last Judge. This last judge of Israel was Samuel. He was both a judge and a prophet. During Samuel's reign as a judge in Israel the people asked for a king.

> And it came to pass, when Samuel was old, that he made his sons judges over Israel. Now the name of his firstborn was Joel; and the name of his second, Abiah: they were judges in Beersheba. And his sons walked not in his ways, but turned aside after lucre, and took bribes, and perverted judgment. Then all the elders of Israel gathered themselves together, and came to Samuel unto Ramah, and said unto him, Behold, you are old, and your sons walk not in your ways: **now make us a king to judge us like all the nations.** But the thing displeased Samuel, when they said, Give us a king to judge us. And Samuel prayed unto YHVH" (1 Sam. 8:1-6).

This question displeased Samuel. At first, it appears that Samuel is upset because they have rejected him and his sons, but when you read further the answer becomes clear. Samuel prayed unto God and the answer received was,

> Hearken unto the voice of the people in all that they say unto thee: **for they have not rejected you, but they have rejected me, that I should not reign over them**. According to all the works which they have done since the day that I brought them up out of Egypt even unto this day, wherewith they have forsaken me, and served other gods, so do they also unto you. Now therefore hearken unto their voice: howbeit yet protest solemnly unto them, and show them the manner of the king that shall reign over them" (1 Sam. 8:7-9).

Samuel was displeased because the people had rejected God as their King. Samuel then warned the people of the king they would have.

> And he said, **this will be the manner of the king that shall reign over you**: He will take your sons, and appoint them for himself, for his chariots, and to be his horsemen; and some shall run before his chariots. And he will appoint him captains over thousands, and captains over fifties; and will set them to ear his ground, and to reap his harvest, and to make his instruments of war, and instruments of his chariots. And he will take your daughters to be confectionaries, and to be cooks, and to be bakers. And he will take your fields, and your vineyards, and your olive yards, even the best of them, and give them to his servants. And he will take the tenth of your seed, and of your vineyards, and give to his officers, and to his servants. And

> he will take your menservants, and your maidservants, and your goodliest young men, and your donkeys, and put them to his work. He will take the tenth of your sheep: and you shall be his servants. And you shall cry out in that day because of your king which you shall have chosen you; and YHVH will not hear you in that day" (1 Sam. 8:11-18).

This king that the people asked for would not be what they expected. This king would do things to take away the people's liberty. This king would take their sons for himself. He would also take their chariots and horsemen. He would also take their daughters to be bakers and cooks. This king would take away their freedoms which the Law of God provides.

America has gone the same path as ancient Israel. Just as colonial America is very similar to the time of the judges, the inauguration of our first president is very similar to the anointing of Israel's first king. Samuel said the king will "take your sons, and appoint them for himself, for his chariots, and to be his horsemen; and some shall run before his chariots" (1 Sam. 8:11). This is a reference to war. The king will build a standing army. America did the same thing. It is simply called the military. American presidents have instituted a standing army and can institute the military draft when needed. Samuel then said, "And he will appoint him captains over thousands, and captains over fifties; and will set them to ear his ground, and to reap his harvest, and to make his instruments of war, and instruments of his chariots" (1 Sam. 8:12). America did the same thing. It is called the military industrial complex working for wages. "The military-industrial complex is a nation's military establishment, as well as the industries involved in the production of armaments and other military materials."[95] America has large businesses providing the government with supplies for military purposes. This is just like ancient Israel when they anointed their first king. They built a standing army and had the people fund that operation. Samuel then said, "he will take your daughters to be confectionaries, and to be cooks, and to be bakers" (1 Sam. 8:13). The king will put women in the work force. The same thing has happened in America. It used to be common for women to be "keepers at home" (Tit. 2:5). The husband would work outside the home to earn a living for the household while the wife would take care of the home and manage the household affairs. This was a great system that worked for America. Now, women have to work in America to afford to pay for our nations needs through the heavy progressive income tax. To be able to afford everything provided by our government, two incomes for every family is almost necessary. Samuel then said, "he will take your fields, and your vineyards, and your olive yards, even the best of them, and give them to his servants" (1 Sam. 8:14). In America this is simply call eminent domain. Eminent domain is, "The power to take private property for public use by the state, municipalities, and private persons or corporations authorized to exercise functions of public character."[96] This is where government can take property for public uses. This removes the rights

---

[95] Military-Industrial Complex, History.com Editors et al., A&E Television Networks, August 21, 2018, https://www.history.com/topics/21st-century/military-industrial-complex.

[96] Black, Henry Campbell, "Eminent Domain." *Black's Law Dictionary*, Fifth Edition, pg. 470.

of the people and gives that right to the public through government. Samuel then said, "he will take the tenth of your seed, and of your vineyards, and give to his officers, and to his servants" (1 Sam. 8:15). In America, this is call the income tax, and it is no longer ten percent. Income tax has varied quite a bit over American history but is currently between ten and thirty-seven percent. This is a much heavier burden than the ten percent tithe that God established.   Finally, Samuel said, "he will take your menservants, and your maidservants, and your goodliest young men, and your donkeys, and put them to his work" (1 Sam. 8:16). This is called Social Security in America today. Social Security is a program where the American people sign over their labor to the government in exchange for all the benefits from the program. See Table 11 for a comparison between Israel and the United States.

Israel	The United States
Take your sons for war (1 Sam 8:11)	Military draft
Take your sons to ear the ground (1 Sam 8:12)	Military industrial complex working for wages
Take your daughters to the work force (1 Sam. 8:13)	Women will leave the home to go to work.
Take your fields for his servants (1 Sam 8:14)	Eminent Domain
Take a tenth of your seed (1 Sam 8:15)	Income Tax
Take your servants and property and put them to his work (1 Sam 8:16)	Social Security

Table 11

As can be seen, America has followed the same route as ancient Israel. Different terms are used today, but it is very similar as ancient Israel. In fact, the next section will demonstrate that America was founded on God's law.

Remember, the Bible is a law book, written in legal code, and deals with national geopolitics. God is dealing with the nations and governments of the world, He is not dealing with the religions of the world. This last section will discuss where God's law is today and how it is practiced in the nations of the world. The Torah's model of government is found throughout the scripture. It goes by several names such as the Elders of Israel, the Levitical Priesthood, or the congregation of Israel (more on this in book two). In the nations of today, however, governments go by different names, but it is the law they practice that matters most.

Where is God's Law Today?

There is often a disconnect with cultures from thousands of years ago to cultures today. It is sometimes difficult to see similarities, especially when it comes to government and legal systems. It seems they did things much differently in ancient times than what is typically done today. Often, this is attributed to religious beliefs, rather than practicality and reason. For example, the concept of tithing in ancient Israel takes on an entirely religious meaning today, but this is not what tithing was to the ancient Israelites. There was a very practical reason for tithing and it had a national purpose. The truth is that while modern times might be much more advanced in the field of industry and technology, the same laws are practiced today that were practiced then. Those laws have just been modified to meet the more advanced society of today. The laws of ancient Israel, the Torah, are still around today, just under a different name. Today the Torah is called, the Common Law. Right now, the reader might be thinking that they have heard of the Common Law, but they are not quite sure what it is. Here are some quotes to demonstrate the history of the Common Law. Chancellor James Kent, who wrote the Commentaries on American Law, was an American jurist, a New York legislator, a legal scholar, and first Professor of Law at Columbia College. He made this statement in an address delivered before The Law Association of New York.

> Happily, for this country, we received our jurisprudence from England in its highest vigour, and in its most cultivated state. The leading statesmen in the colonies, and especially the members of the bar, had the sagacity to perceive, and the courage and patriotism to assert, the indefeasible title of their countrymen to all the securities and blessings of the **English common law**.[97]

The United States of America was founded on the Common Law. To further support this, Henry Campbell Black, who wrote *Black's Law Dictionary*, which is one of the more prominent legal dictionaries of the modern era, said, "It means due process of law warranted by the constitution, **by the common law adopted by the constitution**, or by statutes passed in pursuance of the constitution."[98] The Common Law was adopted by the Constitution of the United States. In fact, nearly a third of the population of the planet lives under a Common Law jurisdiction or a mixture thereof. The question naturally

---

[97] Chancellor James Kent, An Address Delivered Before The Law Association of New York, New-York, G. & C. Carvill & Co., 1836, pg. 14.

[98] Black, Henry Campbell, "Law of the Land." *Black's Law Dictionary*, 2nd Edition, pg. 702, 1910

arises, where does the Common Law come from? Probably the most notable law expert in the past few centuries was Sir William Blackstone, who was mentioned earlier in this book. He was an English jurist and politician from the eighteenth century. He is most known for his work, *Commentaries on the Laws of England*, where he expounded on the English Common Law. In this writing he said,

> This has given manifold occasion for the benign interposition of **divine providence**; which, in compassion to the frailty, the imperfection, and the blindness of human reason, hath been pleased, at sundry times and in divers manners, to discover and enforce its laws by an immediate and direct revelation. **The doctrines thus delivered we call the revealed or divine law, and they are to be found only in the holy Scriptures.**[99]

Sir William Blackstone, one of the most notable legal experts of the past several centuries, attributed the Common Law to be "found only in the holy Scriptures." It was well known in past generations that law comes from the Creator. It is only in modern times that this has been forgotten. This is very unfortunate and a detriment to nations today. When God is not given credit for His work, then His people will forget the many blessings received for their obedience to His law. God's law today is known as the Common Law. The Common Law was founded in the late 880's and early 890's by King Alfred the Great. King Alfred wrote his *Doom Book*, *Dōmbōc*, or *Code of Alfred*. The word "Dōm" in Old English is the word for "judgment"

---

[99] Blackstone, Sir William, Knight, *Commentaries on the Laws of England*, Vol. 1, (The Lawbook Exchange, LTD. Clark, New Jersey, 2011), pg. 31)

and the word "bōc" in Old English is the word for book. This was King Alfred's Judgment Book, or Legal Code. This history of where law comes from is almost forgotten today. God's law, the Torah, is alive and well today in many nations. Unfortunately, those nations have forgotten where that law comes from and have turned to another legal system.

Edward Gibbon was a historian and politician from the eighteenth century. He is most distinguished for his writing, *The History of the Decline and Fall of the Roman Empire*. This six-volume historical account is one of the most extensive historical accounts of the Roman Empire even to this day. In this writing Gibbon said, "The wise Alfred adopted as an indispensable duty the extreme rigor of the Mosaic institutions."[100] The knowledge that the English Common Law came from God was well known in the past. In fact, this history of God's law through England traces back further than King Alfred. King Alfred stood on the shoulders of other kings prior to him. Dunvallo Molmutius was a legendary king of the Britons around 470 to 450 BC. In the historic writing, *History of the Kings of Britain*, by Geoffrey of Monmouth, it was said about Dunvallo Molmutius, "This prince established what the Britons call the Molmutine laws, which are famous among the English to this day."[101] The law that is "famous among the English" is a reference to the Common Law. Another source to show this king's commitment to the Law of God is from Professor Francis Nigel Lee and his book, *Common*

---

[100] Edward Gibbon, *The History of the Decline and Fall of the Roman Empire*, Volume 3, P378

[101] Geoffrey of Monmouth, *History of the Kings of Britain*, translated by Aaron Thompson, pg. 36, 1999

Law: Roots and Fruits. In this writing Lee said, "the British King Dunvall Moelmud proclaimed God's Moral Law (and its judicial applications) to be the Common Law of the land."[102]

The Law of the Land is an interesting study. In the past, the Law of the Land was typically referred to as the Common Law. In America, the Constitution is the Law of the Land, but that same Constitution has adopted the Common law. What then is the Law of the Land? Here are a few quotes to consider. The Law of the Land is "the general law which hears before it condemns, which proceeds upon inquiry, and renders judgment only after trial. The meaning is that every citizen shall hold his life, liberty, property, and immunities under the protection of general rules which govern society. Everything which may pass under the form of an enactment is not the law of the land."[103] This statement from *Black's Law Dictionary* sounds very much like the description of God's law in the Scripture. The Law of the Land is the foundational law of a nation to provide life, liberty, property, and immunities to all of its citizens. In fact, the Scripture even endorses a trial before condemnation so that the individual can defend themselves (Deut. 19:15). What is interesting is the statement, "everything which may pass under the form of an enactment is not the law of the land." This phrase is omitted in later versions of Black's Law Dictionary. An enactment is the "adding to" and "taking away" from God's law that the Scripture warns of (Deut.

---

[102] Rev. Prof. Dr. Adv., Francis Nigel Lee, *COMMON LAW: ROOTS AND FRUITS*, Preface pg. xi, 1997

[103] Black, Henry Campbell, "Law of the Land." *Black's Law Dictionary*, 2nd ed. pg. 702, 1910

4:2). America has the right Law of the Land, but the people sometimes enact legislation contrary to that law. These enactments, over time, become the law of the land for that nation. This is what God warned of. Enactments should always be in accordance with God's law. *Black's Law Dictionary* continues saying, "It means due process of law warranted by the constitution, by the common law adopted by the constitution, or by statutes passed in pursuance of the constitution."[104] The last phrase of this statement is critical. Statutes are to be passed in pursuance of the constitution. Statutes that are passed contrary to the constitution can be dangerous to the life, liberty, property and immunities of that people. This is God warning man to stay the course with His law. If this warning is not heeded, man might erode their own freedoms and liberties.

Due process is also a very important principle of law. As quoted earlier, Henry Campbell Black said, the law of the land "means due process of law warranted by the constitution." Due process of law is, "Law in its regular course of administration through courts of justice."[105] Courts of justice determine what the law of the land is, and this is what the Common Law is. Here is what the Encyclopedia Britannica says about the Common Law. The Common Law is "the body of customary law, **based upon judicial decisions** and embodied in reports of **decided cases**, that has been administered by the common-law

---

[104] Black, Henry Campbell, "Law of the Land." *Black's Law Dictionary*, 2nd ed. pg. 702, 1910

[105] Black, Henry Campbell, "Due Process of Law." *Black's Law Dictionary*, 5th ed. pg. 449, 1979

courts of England since the Middle Ages."[106] The Common Law is the law of England as administered by common law courts. The Common Law can actually be traced all the way back to Moses and the Law of God. In fact, the entirety of King Alfred's codification of the Mosaic Law is found in another writing by Professor Francis Nigel Lee called *King Alfred the Great and our Common Law*. From pages nine through fourteen Professor Lee lists out the Common Law as King Alfred wrote. There are forty-eight dooms (judgments) of the Common Law listed. For each of the forty-eight dooms, Lee listed the scriptural reference. Unfortunately, there is another law that is taking nations away from the Common Law (God's law).

Two Systems of Law:

There are essentially two systems of law working in the nations of today. These two legal systems have many similarities, but it is where they differ that causes problems. The first legal system, as seen in the previous section of this book, is the Common Law, which according to Sir William Blackstone, is "found only in the Holy Scriptures." This is the Law of God found in many nations today. The second, however, is another law that comes from another source. This law is the Roman Civil Law, which is often simply called the Civil Law today. According to Henry Campbell Black, "The 'Roman Law' and the 'Civil Law' are convertible phrases, meaning the same system of

---

[106] Kiralfy, A. Roland , Lewis, . Andrew D.E. and Glendon, . Mary Ann (2024, October 25). common law. Encyclopedia Britannica Online.

jurisprudence."[107] When Americans use the term, "Civil Law" they are referring to the Roman Civil Law. The Civil Law traces from Rome all the way through history and even to modern times. Black further explains about the Civil Law when he says it was, "The system of jurisprudence held and administered in the Roman empire, particularly as set forth in the compilation of Justinian and his successors, . . . as distinguished from the common law of England."[108] The Civil Law has been around for centuries, even since Rome was first established. Although this law traces back to Rome, there is really another source where this law comes from, and that source is the people of the nation. Black continues by saying, "The law which the people enact is called the "Civil Law" of that people, but that law which natural reason appoints for all mankind is called the "law of nations," because all nations use it."[109] The Civil Law today is the "law which the people enact." As a nation grows the people of that nation enact legislation that changes the law.

This sounds eerily familiar. In Deuteronomy 4:2 it says, "You shall not add to the word that I command you, nor take from it, that you may keep the commandments of [YHVH] your God that I command you." (ESV) At first this simply sounds as an appeal to not alter the Holy Scriptures, but that is not what God is saying. The topic of discussion

---

[107] Black, Henry Campbell, "Civil Law." *Black's Law Dictionary*, 2nd Ed., pg. 204, 1910.

[108] Black, Henry Campbell, "Civil Law." *Black's Law Dictionary*, 5th Ed., pg. 223, 1979.

[109] Black, Henry Campbell, "Civil Law." *Black's Law Dictionary*, 2nd Ed., pg. 204, 1910.

is the "commandments of your God." God is saying not to "add" to His commandments nor "take" away from His commandments. The basic understanding of this verse, especially within the context of Deuteronomy, is to not alter or change the commandments of YHVH within the nation of Israel. The Common Law is the Torah in today's world. The Civil Law is the law that is enacted by the people of a nation. This is what God is referring to. Nations are not to change their law away from YHVH's Torah. In America, the Civil Law is the law that is added to our foundational law, which is the Common Law adopted by the Constitution of the United States. The Civil Law has the potential to alter the Law of God within the nations of today. The people now have the power to change God's law within that nation. God is giving man a warning not to "add" to His law or to "take" away from His law. Keep in mind, this writer is not disparaging the Civil Law. Those Civil Laws that support God's law are righteous and good, but those Civil Laws that do not support God's law are very dangerous. The Civil Law should only be used to clarify laws that may not fit in a more modern society. For example, there are no traffic laws in the Scripture for obvious reasons. Traffic laws that fit within the spirit of God's law are perfectly acceptable civil laws today.

This then is the difference between the Common Law and the Civil Law. The Law of God is unchanging and should be the foundational law of all nations. This is the Common Law today; however, the Civil Law should only be used to enact legislation that clarifies God's law for a modern society of today. This can be very dangerous and is the process whereby Common Law nations leave the Law of God to practice something entirely different. It is true that the Civil Law can simply be used to support the Common Law, but that is not always the case. Many times, laws are enacted that take a nation away from the Common Law and Law of God. This is the downfall of a nation. As said earlier in this book, the rise and fall of every nation is based on their obedience to God's law. This is why the Law of God is so important and why when the church stopped teaching it, it was detrimental to that nation. God's law is the foundation of a nation's success. The more a nation keeps the commandments of God, the more success that nation will enjoy. The more a nation breaks the commandments of God, the more that nation will falter. The Scripture simply calls this, "blessings" and "curses." These blessings and curses are found primarily in Leviticus 26 and Deuteronomy 28. God will prosper those nations that keep His commandments, but will discipline a nation that does not.

This is the world today. There are those nations that are founded on God's law and those nations that are not. The nations that are founded on God's law are typically called Common Law nations. They are the nations that embrace freedom and liberty for all their citizens. They have a legal system that is fair and just and protects the rights of its citizens, and these same citizens have the ability to hold their government accountable. The nations that are not founded on God's law tend to gravitate towards socialism and a reliance on their government. Freedom and liberty are not the priority, but a society that puts government and control over people is the priority. This is a society that has a government that regulates every aspect of the society in an attempt to keep everyone equal. This, however, does not provide equality. Equality is simply an equal platform for each individual to succeed. How hard and how smart that individual works will determine their status in their society. Socialism attempts to make everyone equal regardless of how hard or smart they work. Where socialism will reward those who are lazy by giving them equality with those who work hard, God's law provides freedom to all so those who strive to succeed can succeed.

America is an example of a nation that started with God's law, but is now moving towards socialism. Consider the following. Here is a list of the Ten Planks from *The Communist Manifesto* written by Karl Marx. The bullet under each plank shows how America is moving closer and closer to following each plank.

10 Planks of *The Communist Manifesto*:
1. Abolition of private property and the application of all rents of land to public purposes.
   - Property tax, zoning, and the Bureau of Land Management.
2. A heavy progressive or graduated income tax.
   - House Joint Resolution 192 (1933) and the Social Security Act (1936).
3. Abolition of all rights of inheritance.
   - Inheritance Tax, Estate Tax (1916), Probate Laws.
4. Confiscation of the property of all emigrants and rebels.
   - Government seizures, tax liens, Public Law 99:570 (1986)
5. Centralization of credit in the hands of the state, by means of a national bank with State capital and an exclusive monopoly.

- Federal Reserve Bank
6. Centralization of the means of communications and transportation in the hands of the State.
    - Federal Communications Commission (FCC) and the Department of Transportation (DOT)
7. Extension of factories and instruments of production owned by the State; the bringing into cultivation of waste-lands, and the improvement of the soil generally in accordance with a common plan.
    - Corporate capacity, Desert Entry Act, and The Department of Agriculture.
8. Equal liability of all to labor. Establishment of Industrial Armies, Especially for Agriculture.
    - Minimum Wage, Social Security, and the Department of Labor.
9. Combination of agriculture with manufacturing industries, gradual abolition of the distinction between town and country, by a more equitable distribution of population over the country.
    - The Planning Reorganization act (1949), Corporate Farms, Executive Order 11647, Public Law 89-136.
10. Free education for all children in public schools. Abolition of Children's Factory Labor in its Present Form. Combination of Education with Industrial Production.
    - Public, Private, and Home Schooling is regulated by government.[110]

---

[110] Marx Karl and Friedrich Engels, *The Communist Manifesto*, Global Grey ebooks, pg. 23-24, 1848.

This is just an example of how a nation can leave God's law for another. America started out practicing the Law of God, which is called the Common Law. America then started to "add to" and "take from" the Common Law (Deut. 4:2). This was done through Civil Law legislation. Now, America is a much more socialist country than when it started. Of course, if America's legislature only enacted laws in accordance with God's Law, this would not have been a problem. God's warning to not "add to" or "take from" His law is of vital importance. This is why neglecting to study the Torah is detrimental to the nations of this world. This book is a call to pastors and Bible teachers everywhere to teach the importance of keeping God's commandments in the nations of today.

To review, the Common Law is the Torah for nations today. This law is found only in the Holy Scriptures and is practiced by many nations today. Unfortunately, most of these nations today are leaving the Common Law for the Civil Law. This is only a problem when the Civil Law contradicts God's law. In fact, one can argue that it is necessary in today's world and changing times to enact legislation that clarifies God's law for today. If this was as far as nations took the Civil Law, there would be no problem. The point here is a call to action to learn and teach God's law for nations today. God has promised to restore that nation if it does. As 2 Chronicles 7:14 says, "If my people, which are called by my name, shall **humble themselves**, and **pray**, and **seek my face**, and **turn from their wicked ways**; then will I hear from heaven, and will forgive their sin, and will heal their land." Today, many who quote this verse seem willing to do three of the four requirements for God to heal their land. Often, they are willing to humble themselves, pray, and seek His face, but turning from their wicked ways requires a turning back to God's law. So far, this has not been done in America. America needs to humble themselves, pray, seek God's face, and learn and practice the Law of God.

This is the problem in the world today. There are two laws at war with each other. The one law, God's Law (Common Law), provides freedom and liberty for the people of that nation. The other law, man's law, better known as communism or socialism, takes away freedom and liberty from the people of that nation. Today, Common Law nations are leaving their foundation in God's law by enacting legislation that is against God's law. It is this writer's opinion that this war of legal systems will eventually usher in the second coming of the Messiah of Israel.

In this last chapter the entirety of King Alfred's codification of the Mosaic Law is found in another writing by Professor Francis Nigel Lee called *King Alfred the Great and our Common Law*. From pages nine through fourteen Professor Lee lists out the Common Law as King Alfred wrote it. This writing concludes with this one final statement. God's law, the Torah, is still alive and well today. Unfortunately, Common Law nations are leaving that law for another law. They should heed the warning of YHVH and "not add to the word that I command you, nor take from it, that you may keep the commandments of YHVH your God that I command you" (Deut. 4:2 – ESV).

The Common Law:

Here is King Alfred's Common Law from *King Alfred the Great and our Common Law* by Professor Nigel Lee. The scriptural references are provided as well.

> The Lord spoke these words to Moses, and said: 'I am the Lord your God. I led you out of the lands and out of the bondage of the Egyptians."

1. Do not love other strange gods before Me! Exodus 20:3
2. Do not call out My Name in idleness! For you are not guiltless with Me, if you call out My Name in idleness. Exodus 20:7
3. Mind that you hallow the rest-day! You must work six days; but on the seventh you must rest! For in six days Christ made Heavens and Earth, the seas, and all the shapen things in them; but He rested on the seventh day. Therefore, the Lord hallowed it. Exodus 20:8-11
4. Honour your father and your mother whom the Lord gave you — so that you may live longer on Earth! Exodus 20:12
5. Do not slay! Exodus 20:13
6. Do not commit adultery! Exodus 20:14
7. Do not steal! Exodus 20:15
8. Do not witness falsely! Exodus 20:16
9. Do not unrighteously desire your neighbour's goods! Exodus 20:17
10. Do not make gold or silver gods for yourself! Exodus 20:4-6
11. These are the judgments which you must appoint. If anyone buys a Christian slave [or man in bondage], let him be bonded for six years — but the seventh, he must freely be unbought. With such clothes as

he went in, with such must he go forth. If he himself had a wife [previously] — she must go out with him. However, if his overlord gave him a wife — she and her bairn [must] go to the overlord. If, however, the bondsman then says, 'I do not wish to go away from my overlord; nor from my wife; nor from my bairn; nor from my goods' — let his overlord then bring him to the door of the church and drill his ear through with an awl, as a sign that he should be a bondsman ever since! Exodus 21:2-6

12. Though anyone sells his daughter as a maidservant, let her not at all be a bondswoman like other women. Nor may he sell her to foreigners. But if he who bought her does not respect her — let her go free, [even] among foreigners. If, then, he [her overlord] allows his son to cohabit with her — let him give her marriage-gifts, and see to it that she receives clothes and the dowry which is the value of her maidenhood! Let him give her that! If he do none of these things to her — then she is free. See: Exodus 21:7f.

13. The man who intentionally slays another man — let him suffer death [Genesis 9:5-6]! He, however, who slay him out of necessity or unwillingly or involuntarily — as when God may have sent him into his power, and when he had not lain in wait for him — he is worthy of his living and lawful fine, if he [the involuntary manslaughterer] seeks asylum. But if any one presumptuously and wilfully slays his neighbour through guile — drag him from

My altar, so that he should suffer death! See: Numbers 35:11-33.

14. He who smites his father or his mother — shall suffer death! Exodus 21:15.

15. He who steals a Freeman and sells him, and it be proved against him, so that he cannot clear himself — let him suffer death! Exodus 21:6

16. If any one smites his neighbour with a stone or with his fist — if he [the one smitten] may go forth, even though only with the help of a staff: get him medicine; and do his work for him, while he himself cannot! See: Exodus 21:12-16.

17. He who smites his own bondservant or bondswoman — if he or she does not die the same day but still lives for two or three nights — he is not at all so guilty [of death]: for it was his own chattel. However, if he or she die the same day — put the guilt upon him [the overlord] See: Exodus 21:20-21.

18. If anyone, while fighting, hurt a pregnant woman — let him pay a fine for the hurt, as the evaluators determine! If she die — let him pay soul with soul! See: Exodus 21:22-23.

19. If anyone puts out another's eye, let him give his own for it: tooth for tooth, hand for hand, foot for foot, burning for burning, wound for wound, stripe for stripe! See: Ex. 21:24-25.

20. If anyone smite out the eye of his manservant or his maidservant, so that he makes them one-eyed — for that, he must free them! See: Exodus 21:26-27.

21. If an ox gores a man or a woman so that they die — let the ox be stoned to death; but do not let its flesh be eaten! The owner is guiltless — if the ox gored two or three days earlier and the owner did not know about it. However, if he did know about it, and if he did not want to impound it — and if it then slew either a man or a woman — let it be destroyed with stones, and let the owner of the slain or the gored bondsman be paid whatever the Council finds to be right! If it gore a son or a daughter, it is worthy of the same judgment. However, if it gored a bondsman or bondsmen, let thirty shillings of silver be given to the overlord; and let the ox be destroyed with stones! See: Exodus 21:28-32.

22. If anyone digs a water-pit; or unties a tied-up animal, and does not tie it up again — let him pay for whatever falls therein; and let him have the dead one! See: Exodus 21:33-34.

23. If an ox wounds another man's ox so that it dies, let them sell the [live] ox and share its value — and, similarly, also the meat of the dead one! However, if the owner knew that the ox was goring, but did not wish to restrain it — let him give another ox for it, and keep all the meat for himself! See: Exodus 21:35-36.

24. If anyone steals another's ox, and slays or sells it — let him give two for it; and four sheep for one! If he does not have anything to give — let he himself be sold for the fee! See: Exodus 22:1.

25. If a thief breaks into a man's house at night, and he be slain there — he [the slayer] is not guilty of manslaughter! If he does this after sun-rise, he is guilty of manslaughter; and he himself shall then die — unless he slew out of necessity! If he [the thief] be caught red-handed with what he previously stole — let him pay twofold for it! See: Exodus 22:2-4.

26. If anyone harms another man's vineyard or his acres or any of his lands — let him pay the fine as men value it! See: Exodus 22:5.

27. If fire be kindled to burn right — let him who tindered the fire then pay a fine for the mischief! Here, for fine Alfred uses the Anglo-Saxon word bot (compare the word 'booty'). See: Exodus 22:6.

28. If anyone entrust livestock to his friend — if he [the friend] himself steals it, let him pay for it twofold! If he does not know who stole it, let him clear himself [from the accusation] that he committed a fraud! However, if it were quick [alias 'live'] cattle — and if he says that the army took it; or that it died of itself; and if he has a witness — he need not pay for it. If he, however, has no witness — and if he [the loser of the livestock] does not believe him [the custodian] — let him then swear! See: Exodus 22:7-11.

29. If anyone deceives an unwedded woman and sleeps with her, let him pay for her — and have her afterwards as his wife! However, if the woman's father does not want to let her go — let him [the seducer]

give money, according to her dowry! Cf. Exodus 22:16-17.

30. Don't let women live who are wont to receive enchanters and conjurers and witches! See: Exodus 22:18. Note: these sorcerers and practitioners of witchcraft were usually also murderers and/or kidnappers.

31. Let him who has intercourse with cattle, suffer death! See: Exodus 22:19. Note: modern departures from the capital punishments in this and other similar provisions here, are departures not just from the Ancient Common Law — but also from the Holy Bible.

32. Also let him who offers sacrifices to the gods — except to God alone — suffer death! See: Exodus 22:18-20. Note: the cruel earlier extermination by (degenerate) unitarian Judaists or Moslems and also by polytheistic Pagans even of private worshippers of the Triune Jehovah as the one and only True God — is here replaced by the humane judicial punishment according to (regenerate) Trinitarian Law not of those who are private but rather of those who are public worshippers of false gods.

33. You must not vex strangers and those who come from afar — for you were strangers, long ago, in the land of the Egyptians! See: Exodus 22:21. Note: not the unitarian mediaeval Jews but the trinitarian Anglo-Britons are here regarded as the legal continuation of the Ancient Israelites.

34. You must not scathe widows and step-children, nor harm them anywhere!

However, if you do otherwise — they cry out to Me, and I hear them; and then I slay you with My sword. Thus I make your wives to be widows, and your bairns to be stepchildren! See: Exodus 22:22-24.

35. If you give money as a loan to your comrade who wants to dwell with you — do not pressure him as one in need; and do not oppress him with interest! See: Exodus 22:25.

36. If a man has nothing but a single garment with which to cover himself or to wear, and he gives it as a pledge — before the sun sets, give it back to him! If you do not do so — he calls out to Me; and I hear him. For I am very mild-hearted. See: Exodus 22:26-27.

37. You may not revile your Lord; nor curse the overlord of the people! See: Exodus 22:28.

38. Your tithe-monies and your first-fruits of things that go, and things that grow — you must give to God! See: Exodus 22:29-30.

39. You may not eat at all of that meat which wild animals leave! Give it to the hounds! See: Exodus 22:31.

40. Do not listen to the words of a liar; nor permit his judgments; nor speak to anyone who gives testimony in his favour! See: Exodus 23:1f.

41. Do not, beyond your right reason, wend yourself to people who are unwise and unrighteous in their wishes, when they speak and cry out — nor to the learning of the most unwise! Do not permit them! See: Exodus 23:2f.

42. If another man's stray cattle come into your power — though it be your foe — make it known to him! See: Exodus 22:4f.

43. You must judge very evenly; do not give one judgment to the wealthy, [but] another to the poor! Nor give one judgment to the more beloved — and another to the more disliked! See: Exodus 23:6.

44. Always shun lies [alias 'Shun thou aye leasings']!

45. You must never slay a righteous [alias 'sooth-fast'] and unguilty man!

46. You must never accept bribes [alias 'meed-monies']! For they all too often blinden wise men's thoughts and turn their words aside. See: Exodus 23:7-8.

47. Do not act in any way uncouthly toward the stranger from abroad [alias 'out-comer']; nor oppress him with any unrighteousness [alias 'uncouthly']!

48. Never swear by heathen gods; nor may you call out to them, in any way! Ex. 23:9.[111]

---

[111] Rev. Prof. Dr. F.N. Lee, *KING ALFRED THE GREAT AND OUR COMMON LAW*, Department of Church History, Queensland Presbyterian Theological Seminary, Brisbane, Australia, August 2000, pg. 9-14

Bibliography:

Barclay, William, *New Testament Words*. Louisville Kentucky, Westminster John Knox Press, 1974.

Barnes, Albert, *Barnes New Testament Notes*. Grand Rapids, Michigan. Baker Book House, 1949.

Black, Henry Campbell, *Black's Law Dictionary*. Fifth Edition, St. Paul, Minnesota, West Publishing CO., 1979.

Blackstone, Sir William, Knight, *Commentaries on the Laws of England*. Philadelphia, Geo. T. Bisel CO., 1922.

Bouvier, John. *A Law Dictionary Adapted to the Constitution and Laws of the United States of America*. Vol. II, Philadelphia, T. and J.W. Johnson, 1839.

Brown Francis, D.D. Litt.D, Driver S.R. D.D. Litt.D, and Briggs Charles, D.D. Litt.D, *The Brown-Driver-Briggs Hebrew and English Lexicon*. Hendrickson Publishers Marketing, LLC, 2012.

Chancellor James Kent, "An Address Delivered Before The Law Association of New York." New-York, G. & C. Carvill & Co., 1836.

Clark, Adam, Clarks's Commentary, New Testament, Vol 6A Romans - Colossians, Books For The Ages, AGES Software, Albany, OR USA, 1996. Version 2.0.

Easton, M.G. M.A., D.D. *Easton's Bible Dictionary*. Third Edition, Books For The Ages, AGES Software, Albany, OR, USA Version 2.0, 1996-1997.

Gill, John, *John Gill's Exposition of the Bible*. New Testament, https://sacred-texts.com/bib/cmt/gill/index.htm.

History.com Editors, et al., Military-Industrial Complex, History.com, A&E Television Networks, Updated: August 21, 2018, https://www.history.com/topics/21st-century/military-industrial-complex.

Geoffrey of Monmouth, *History of the Kings of Britain*. Translated by Aaron Thompson, with revisions by J.A. Giles, Publications Medieval Latin Series, Cambridge, Ontario, 1999.

Josephus, Flavius, *The Works of Josephus*. Translated by William Whiston, A.M., Hendrickson Publishers Inc. 1987.

Kiralfy, Albert Roland , Lewis, Andrew D.E. and Glendon, Mary Ann. "common law". Encyclopedia Britannica, 25 Oct. 2024, https://www.britannica.com/topic/common-law.

Lee, Francis Nigel, Rev. Prof. Dr. Adv. *KING ALFRED THE GREAT AND OUR COMMON LAW*. D.C.L Doctoral Dissertation, Samuel Rutherford School of Law Florida, U.S.A., Vastly expanded from lectures given in June 1985 at the Dallas Conference on Christian Government, Revised 1997.

Lee, Francis Nigel, Rev. Prof. Dr. Adv. *COMMON LAW: ROOTS AND FRUITS*. Department of Church History, Queensland Presbyterian Theological Seminary, Brisbane, Australia, August 2000.

Spiro, Ken, "Crash Course in Jewish History. From Abraham to Modern Israel" Targum Press Inc., 2010.

Strong, James, S.T.D., LL.D. *A Concise Dictionary of the Words in the Hebrew Bible*. Abington Press, Nashville, New York, 1890.

Strong, James, S.T.D., LL.D. *A Concise Dictionary of the Words in the Greek Bible*. Abington Press, Nashville, New York, 1890.

Thayer, Joseph H., *Thayer's Greek - English Lexicon of the New Testament*. Hendrickson Publishers Marketing, LLC, Peabody Massachusetts, 11th ed. 2014.

The Ante-Nicene Fathers: Translations of the Writings of the Fathers Down to A.D. 325. Edited by Alexander Roberts and James Donaldson. 10 vols. 1885–1887.

Gibbon, Edward, *The History of the Decline and Fall of the Roman Empire*. ed. J.B. Bury with an Introduction by W.E.H. Lecky, New York: Fred de Fau and Co., 1906, in 12 vols. Vol. 3.

Thoreau, Henry David, *On the Duty of Civil Disobedience*. Salt Lake City, Utah, Libertas Institute, 1849.

Washington, George. "Washington's Inaugural Address", https://www.archives.gov/milestone-documents/president-george-washingtons-first-inaugural-speech, April 30, 1789.

Wex Definitions Team, Wex Legal Information Institute, Cornell Law School, August of 2022, https://www.law.cornell.edu/

Zodhiates, Spiros Th.D., *The Complete Word Study Dictionary New Testament*, Chattanooga, TN, AMG Publishers, 1993.